More Humor Around Horses

Stu Campbell

Illustrations by R. Loren Schmidt

The author wishes to thank and gratefully acknowledge
Tom Coblentz *and* **The Elkhorn Art Gallery,**
*Winter Park, Colorado, for the use of the oil painting on the cover
and the illustrations used in this book, which were
created by R. Loren Schmidt.*

Copyright © 2013 by Stu Campbell

ISBN 978-0-9675164-6-2

Cover and text design by D.K. Luraas

Printed and bound in the United States of America

Contents

Other Titles by the Author

A Real Horse Outfit?

I didn't have a job one summer. I figured it wouldn't be too hard to find one, as there were a lot of horse outfits around Estes Park, Colorado. I turned down a couple of job offers for various reasons—there wasn't enough pay, living conditions weren't as good as they could have been, or whatever.

I did hire on at one outfit, and I don't want to mention their name for the reasons that follow. The people were sure nice and I really don't want to hurt anyone's feelings, but I had a hard time fitting in.

In other positions that I'd held on horse outfits I'd worked for, I'd managed to adapt to each outfit's way of doing things. Where I had been involved in management and been responsible for training new help, I always let the new help know that if we did a few things different than what they were used to, that they were to do it our way.

I would generally say, "The mark of a good hand is to be able to go to a new outfit and adapt to their way an' get the job done. The end result being to do the chore at hand the way the boss wants it done. There's not much difference between the outfits anyway. Most differences arise from the facilities on the places themselves."

On the outfit I hired on to, the facilities weren't that different. The procedures were. I began to have doubts about my working there before the first day was over.

I got there a little after noon on Sunday and was given a walk through the barn by the owner, and started right to work. Only there weren't any rides scheduled to go out. We spent the afternoon visiting in front of the barn.

When we unsaddled, I asked the name of the horse I unsaddled, found his saddle rack in the tack room and placed it there. I noticed that the saddles had all been oiled and were in pretty good shape. However, the latigos on all the saddles had also been oiled. I don't like that—it makes the latigos hard to pull tight and hard to loosen. As I left to unsaddle another horse, the boss lady said, "We take the bridles off the saddles at night and hang them on the horse's rack in this room." She led the way into another room and showed me the horse's rack, then smiled approvingly as she took the bridle and hung it on the appropriate rack.

My question was, "Why?"

"That's the way we've always done it." The reply was matter of fact, as if it was done that way everywhere.

I couldn't see any rhyme or reason to the procedure. If a horse's bridle is kept with the saddle, there can't be a mix-up. Removing the bridle from the saddle at night just seemed to add to the work and allowed the possibility of getting the wrong bridle on the wrong horse. I didn't say anything, but did it the boss's way, trying to figure out in my mind, *Why?*

When all the horses were unsaddled, they were led to the night pasture, about a hundred yards away, two at a time and turned loose. There was a lot of on foot walking on that place, more than I had anticipated. I noticed that no one kept in a jingle horse. I should have suspected something was different when I

noticed that everyone was wearing hiking boots or walking boots rather than cowboy boots. I noticed it, but didn't pay any attention to it. I thought it was a matter of personal preference.

"Do you like walking in those?" The boss lady noticed my cowboy boots.

"No," I said, "But it's all I got. The only lace-up footwear I have are my golf shoes and a pair of winter boots."

"You might want to wear your golf shoes."

I couldn't believe the boss lady was suggesting I wear golf shoes to ride and work in! I started to have doubts about this being a horse outfit and began to wonder how long I could last here.

"I only wear my golf shoes when I play golf," I said.

There was one other hand on this outfit, and a lot of volunteer help. Pat worked on a neighboring place and showed up two days a week. Rich was supposed to work six days a week.

The next morning, everyone was present and we set out to gather the horses from the night pasture, on foot. I knew I'd made a mistake as I walked through the field and the morning dew on the grass slowly seeped through my boots onto my feet. And there were some boggy spots in the pasture.

Someone had caught a horse and was leading him to the barn. The rest of the horses were following; some at a trot and some at a slow lope. The boss lady had put out some grain in the barn and there was a lot of confusion in the barn as the horses jockeyed for position to get the grain. Amongst the confusion, the boss lady was trying to halter the horses and tie them in the stalls.

There was more confusion. There were only eight stalls and there were twelve horses. I followed the horses to the barn and started to halter those that weren't haltered. There was more confusion.

Each horse had his own halter, designated by color. There weren't any nametags on the halters. Some of the horses were tied outside the barn and grained in a rubber tub. A person needed to have a good memory to work here and do things the boss lady's way.

Saddling was another matter. There wasn't enough room in the stalls to throw saddles and the rafters inside the barn were low. I saddled one horse in the barn, and then started to saddle horses outside the barn. At least there was room to work.

Each horse had his own blanket and pad. Some pads had the horse's name on them, some didn't, and some had other horses names on them, but weren't being used because the horses that had used them had died. The whole mess was very confusing to me.

When all the horses were saddled, I was curtly reminded that we had to put the bridles on the saddles. "Oh, yes," I said, "we took 'em off last night." I still haven't figured out the reasoning behind that; it led to a lot of extra walking that I wasn't enjoying in wet boots and socks.

I haven't yet figured out the reasoning behind removing the bridles from the saddles. Trying to make sense out of the situation, the only plausible reason I can come up with is that the saddle racks were only made of a two-by-four nailed to the wall. With the cinch slung up over the seat of the saddle and the bridle on the near side of the saddle, the saddle might become lopsided and fall off the rack. I would have put a cinch keeper on the off side of the saddle and used that. This would have kept the saddle balanced and eliminated the need to take the bridles off the saddles at night and put them back on in the morning. However, I didn't say anything; that was their system, and they'd been doing it that way for years.

We had a five-hour ride that morning that was supposed to leave at nine o'clock. There was a mom and her ten-year-old son and a fourteen-year-old daughter. The riders showed up at nine-thirty, and by the time they got their sun screen and long pants on, they didn't leave until after ten.

Pat was scheduled to take the ride and I thought Rich was going to go, to learn the trails. He had been there longer than I had. But when Rich was asked to go, his comment was, "I don't want to ride!"

I thought that was kinda strange. He was certainly in the wrong business if he didn't want to ride. I volunteered to go along just to learn the trails.

Pat took along an axe and a small saw to clear the trail if necessary and we started out. I didn't much like crossing the road with three tourists, but we did it and we got into the forest. I didn't really think much of the trail; a lot of trees and not the vast, panoramic view I expected to see occasionally.

Towards the end of the trail there were a couple of trees down over the trail. Pat's horse just stepped over the first tree, but the boy's horse jumped it and he almost fell off. I had to holler at Pat to have him keep an eye on the ride.

We proceeded to our destination point, got the riders off and let them eat their lunch.

Before we started back, the boy asked Pat, "Can we go around that tree on the way back?"

Pat nodded a yes and we started out. When we reached the fallen tree, Pat's horse stepped over it, the boy's horse stepped over it, but the mom's horse jumped it. She almost fell off.

I had to holler at Pat again to watch the ride. This time he stopped.

"We better do something about that," said Pat. He got off his horse, took out the axe and cut the end of the tree.

Strange, I thought, *we almost nearly lose two people, then he fixes the situation.* I came to the conclusion that Pat didn't have much regard for the safety of the riders.

The ride back to the stables wasn't very enjoyable for the guests. It was mostly downhill and Pat's horse set a fast pace going home; so fast that the other horses had to trot to keep up. I had to holler at Pat more than once to slow down. I thought we might have one of the riders fall off at a trot. But we made it home without incident.

After the riders left, I thought that the young boy might have a hard time sitting down for supper. He was bound to have a sore butt from all the bouncing he'd done on the trip home.

The end of the day was the same as the day before, unsaddling, taking bridles off saddles. Before we were done, I had concluded that I really didn't want to work on this place.

When the horses were unsaddled, the boss lady came out with some money in her hand. "This is the tip money we made today," she said. "We split the tips with everyone at the end of the day."

She split the tips equally among the three of us. Rich, who didn't go on a ride, shared in the bounty. I thought this was kinda strange and it cut my share down considerably.

Rich was a different matter. He didn't want to ride and didn't show much interest in learning the trails. He had been the manager at a lodge that had been sold and the new management was scaling back their horse operations. Apparently he wanted to be the barn boss and didn't want to do much of anything. He did want to take a nap every day about ten-thirty.

However, he did have to clean the barn while the rides were out. I didn't think that was too hard, especially when all the horses were gone. There wasn't any manure to clean up!

From his actions and some of his comments, I thought he might have some thoughts about quitting. I had already made up my mind to leave and had set two goals. The first goal was to leave before Rich, as I didn't want to leave the boss lady short-handed, and the second goal was to get Rich horseback! It wouldn't bother me because according to this outfit's policy, I could still make some tip money even if I didn't go out on a ride!

Our procedure for unsaddling was the same that night and the horses were led down to the night pasture. I decided to try and figure out some scheme to get out of gathering the night pasture on foot the next morning. All I could come up with was to show up a few minutes late for work the next day. I did, but it didn't work; they were all waiting for me when I showed up.

"Guess my watch is runnin' a little slow," I said. That should be a good excuse; there wasn't a clock on the place that showed the right time.

We started to gather the pasture and the horses were coming in for their grain. The boss lady was in the barn trying to halter the horses and put them in the proper stall. She was actually creating more problems than she was solving and most of the time she was simply in the way.

There was only one ride scheduled for the day, a one-hour ride, and the boss lady took it out. I thought Rich would go along to learn the trail, but he was content to stay at the barn. The boss lady asked me if I wanted to go, and I said yes. I hadn't told her I was leaving and didn't want to spring the news too early.

The ride proved to be uneventful and the boss lady was a walking encyclopedia of facts about the area and the flowers and such. She rarely stopped talking and when she did, it wasn't for very long.

I learned the one-hour trail, although it went through a cabin area. When the ride was over, the people paid and other than unsaddling, we were done for the day, except for one little chore.

The boss lady sat down to visit with one of her neighbors, who was also a volunteer helper, and sent Rich and me out to clean a ditch.

I grabbed a rake and Rich grabbed a shovel and we set out to clean a ditch that ran from one pond to another. Apparently there was some irrigating involved with this job!

I was getting a little more discouraged each minute I cleaned the ditch.

When we got done and back to the barn, I got the boss lady off to the side and said, "There have been some opportunities that have come up since I checked my phone messages, and I need to check them out. I figure I'll help you out tomorrow, then help you saddle Sunday morning, then leave. I'll bring my truck down here, load my stuff an' we can settle up."

She looked hurt when I told her I was leaving.

"Is there anything I can do to get you to stay?"

"I don't think so," I replied. "These opportunities only come around every so often, and whether or not they pan out, I've got to check them out. I know it's a gamble, but I really need to do it."

The boss lady didn't say anything else.

I was elated! The end was in sight!

The rest of the day was uneventful and we unsaddled and led the horses to the night pasture. I was still not in the habit of taking the bridles off the saddles and hanging them in the other room. But I was content knowing I only had one more day to work.

In the morning, the boss lady had a unique plan.

"Why don't you stay at the barn and regulate the horses?"

"You want me to regulate the horses?" I was somewhat startled at her suggestion.

"Yes," she replied.

"It's pretty hard to regulate the horses when they're in a hurry to get their grain," I said. "Don't put out the grain until after the horses are haltered and tied in their stalls. There's bound to be some fighting between the horses and this action will alleviate some of it."

The boss lady had some other comment, but I cut her off.

"Rich is bringin' them in now."

Without regulation, the horses entered the barn and corral and sorted themselves out. The grain was put out and we started saddling.

Imagine that, I thought, *the boss lady wanting me to "regulate" those horses! Stand right in the way of a bunch of horses runnin' in to get their grain! I don't think I'm quite ready to commit suicide! Yes, I'm ready to leave this place!*

There was only one ride scheduled for that day, a one-hour ride.

The boss lady asked, "Who wants to go?"

I remained silent, knowing I was leaving the next morning. But I did point to Rich.

"Come and go with me, Rich," said the boss lady. "You can learn the trail."

Reluctantly, Rich got a horse, we got the dudes horseback, and they left and I was alone. I did have some manure to clean up, but didn't have anything else to do. I thought a relaxing afternoon before I left to check out my other opportunities might be sorta nice. And I would get to share in the tips, if there were any! The closer we got to the end of the day, the more I was enjoying this job and was actually looking forward to packing my things and leaving the next morning. I was really in a good mood.

We unsaddled that night and much to my amazement, I remembered to take off all the bridles and hang them on their rack. I was in an exceptionally good mood!

I helped saddle the next morning, got my truck loaded, got paid and left.

I'm always glad when the end of a season comes. I'm generally tired and ready to move on. But when I left this outfit, I was elated and even overjoyed after only working six days!

Yes, I know that the mark of a good hand when going to a new outfit is that you adapt to their way of doing things. The different mannerisms on this outfit made me wonder, *Maybe I'm too old to change or maybe I'm not as good a hand as I thought I was!*

Author's note: I was almost as glad to be done writing this as I was to be leaving that outfit!

The New Horse

Dave bought a new horse. The horse wasn't very big, just a little over fourteen hands. He was built pretty well, a palomino gelding, but I wasn't sure what Dave's intentions were with him.

Dave buys a lot of horses for our rental horse business at Moraine Park Stables in Rocky Mountain National Park in Colorado. I didn't know whether the horse was going to be used in our dude string or if it was for his personal use. Dave will buy a few horses for himself during the summer, do some training on them, and sell them during the winter in Phoenix, Arizona.

I know its impolite to come right out and ask a feller what he paid for a new horse and I've heard some of the hired help ask him what he had to give for a horse. The college-age kids we hire for the summer aren't really familiar with the politeness of the older cowboys. These inquiries are generally answered with a curt, "Plenty," or a "Haw," or totally ignored.

I'm not really interested in the price of a horse. All my life people have paid me to ride their horses or they've paid me to ride my horses. But I had ways of finding out Dave's intentions without coming right out and asking him.

"Pretty nice lookin' horse for a dude horse," I said, as Dave haltered him to put him in with his personal horses. He'd got home after dark and turned the horse loose in an empty pen for the night.

My comment was met with a hearty, "Haw!" That response told me the horse was for Dave's own use.

"This horse isn't a dude horse!" Dave acted like I'd insulted him. "This is a reining prospect!"

Knowing that the horse was for his own use, I replied, "It's nice to see you're finally buyin' some horses you can get on without havin' to use a mountin' block or findin' a log or rock to help you!"

Dave has always leaned toward buying big horses, usually sixteen hands or bigger. Of course he always had a use for them.

I suspect Dave is probably a few years younger than I am, although he claims he's not, he won't tell me, but we're both old enough where it's getting more difficult to get on the bigger horses. I've yet to see him use the mounting block, but I have seen him using a log or a rock to get on his horse. I have not stooped so low as to use the mounting block, but I always have the horse standing down hill from me when I get on. And I'll use a rock or a log to help me get on when I'm out on the trail and I'm sure nobody's looking.

On our dude rides, I'll get off my horse to check cinches or pick up a dropped item for a guest. When it's time to remount, I'll make a big deal of looking around for a rock, about the size of a silver dollar, placing it in the proper spot, standing on it, then getting on my horse. Our guests that are a little familiar with horses find this kinda humorous, as a lot of them have horses and face the same problems getting on. A lot of the tourists don't have a clue as to what I'm doing.

I'm often reminded of the old cowboy who said, "All my life I've wanted to buy and own those big, stout, good lookin' horses, but never could afford it. Now that I can afford to buy those big horses, I can't get on 'em!" I think of that old boy every time I have to get on a big horse.

"Well, you certainly ought to be able to get on him easy," I said. "That's got to be a prime consideration, especially at our age!"

My last comment was a weakly disguised attempt to allow me to ride the horse. But it went either unnoticed or ignored because there wasn't a response.

"This guy is going to Phoenix for further training," Dave said. "I've got a friend down there that is a reining-horse trainer and I think he can bring this horse along. Then I'll show him some and sell him."

I knew my chances of riding the horse had gone down the drain.

"He's probably a big, tall lanky guy that won't have a problem getting' on him," I said.

"Yep," replied Dave.

"I didn't know you were into reinin' horses," I said.

"Oh yes," replied Dave. "That paint horse is a reining prospect."

"Where are you gonna work the horse up here? There are too many rocks around here to tune up a reinin' horse."

"That's why he's going to Phoenix."

"You mean to tell me that you bought a horse for someone else to ride?"

"No," answered Dave. "I'll ride him in the shows."

"Will you call me when you're showin' him? I'd like to see that."

"No." Dave's reply was short.

"You don't want anybody watchin' when the horse turns out from under you?"

Grinning, Dave said, "No. But I do get dizzy riding these reining horses when they spin."

"Call me when you show the horse. I'd like to see both events."

"Both events?"

"Yeah," I said. "The horse spinnin' an' you fallin' off!"

"Haw!"

"I bet you don't call," I said. I knew Dave wasn't much on drawing attention to himself.

"No, I won't. I'd hate to see you have too much fun at my expense!"

Confusion

New help at our riding stable have to go through some fairly intensive training. Being the barn boss, I'm in charge of doing the training and it usually consists of showing how to saddle and bridle the horses, getting the new help to mount properly and telling them what to say, plus a lot of other things that the new hands should already know.

Most of the new hands are already familiar with the procedures, but our training sessions are good to show them how we want it done. It serves as a good reminder for them. Then, of course, some of our new hands don't have a clue as to how to do what we want done. These training sessions become an intense learning experience for some of these relatively inexperienced hands.

On top of our training sessions, the rangers at Rocky Mountain National Park conduct a training session for all concessionaires conducting business within the national park. These sessions are mandatory and usually consist of such things as what to do in case of an emergency; specific answers to the most commonly asked questions by the tourists; identification of plants and animals and a few warnings about park regulations, edible plants and, of course, a warning about not drinking the water in the streams. The water in the mountain streams can cause giardia, a condition that causes stomach cramps and diarrhea. The Park Service's training is accompanied by a manual that goes into further detail because of time restraints during the training session. But they do cover a lot of information. Digesting this information can be kinda difficult, particularly if a person wants to get it right.

Such was the case with Lindsey. She was a tall, nice looking gal from back East somewhere, I can't remember where, and a college student. Her horsemanship skills were good, as she had her own horses and had even broke and trained a few colts. Her desire to excel was unsurpassed.

That may have been what caused her some problems, not serious, more humorous, but still problems.

Lindsey guided a large ride one morning, large enough that I had to send two extra guides along to help out. There was a Japanese family on this ride that spoke very limited English. I put this family in the line right behind Lindsey so she could keep a close eye on them and try to communicate as well as possible with them. I also alerted the other guides to the fact that there might be some communication problems on this ride and they were to stay alert.

Apparently the ride went well. When they returned, everyone was smiling and laughing, even the Japanese family. I was relieved to see this; sometimes communication can become a problem with foreigners if something should happen. The tourists even made comments to me, like, "That was a great ride!" and "That ride was the most fun we've had on this trip!"

When the tourists had all left, the laughing continued among the guides.

Curious, I asked the guides, "What's goin' on?"

"Ask Lindsey," replied one guide.

"Tell her to be sure not to drink the water!"

This reply heightened my curiosity more. "I still don't understand what's happenin'."

"Just ask Lindsey."

Apparently nobody wanted to tell me what had happened and Lindsey was starting to blush. I had to get to the bottom of this!

"Pat," I ordered, "come over here and tell me what happened!"

"All right," Pat said, "but come over here and I'll tell you."

We moved away from the group about twenty yards so Pat could speak in relative confidence. I could tell Pat was a little uncomfortable describing the event.

"You know how Lindsey is so particular about getting everything right?"

"Yeah," I replied.

"Well, Lindsey was telling about the park, what to do and what not to do, and …" Pat started laughing.

The other hands, about twenty yards away, started laughing also.

"Go on." I was getting a little perturbed that I wasn't getting the information I wanted.

"Lindsey," continued Pat, "told them not to drink the water because they'd get gonorrhea!" Pat broke up and started laughing more. "She got giardia and gonorrhea confused!"

I started laughing. "What did the tourists say?"

"The Japanese family didn't say anything. They didn't understand. But the folks behind them did! They thought it was funny!"

"I imagine it was." I was still laughing.

That afternoon, I had to send Lindsey on another ride. As I told her to get her horse, I added, "Make sure you take some *bottled* water along!"

Lindsey blushed, got her horse and started her ride. As she left, almost all the hands cordially reminded her to take "some *bottled* water along!"

Lindsey blushed quite a bit the next couple of days; a person might have thought she'd got too much sun! But after a few days, the humor at her expense died down.

Of course everyone watched a little closer the way they chose their words with the dudes. And they were careful to make sure they had bottled water!

Jason

Jason was from Georgia and came to work for us in the spring of 2008, I think. It's hard to remember all the details exactly. He was a big guy, not really much taller than I am, but broader and a lot stouter. He was pretty much all muscle, built like a football linebacker. I remember thinking that he would be nice to have around and sorta make the hard work easier on me.

Jason's horsemanship skills were not really all that good. Like most kids, he had done some riding, but he hadn't really done enough to become an accomplished or greatly experienced horseman. But, with a summer at Moraine Park Stables guiding tourist rides through Rocky Mountain National Park, he would have the opportunity to improve his skills.

He had tried to do some rodeoing, but wasn't too successful. Bull riding appealed to him, probably because of the "macho" image it presented. He had a big scar on the inside of one of his legs as the result of an unsuccessful attempt to make the eight seconds and was gored.

Jason reminded me of a friend of my son, Will, in Grand County, Colorado. Doug Baker was big, like Jason. Doug wanted to ride bareback broncs in the rodeo, but he was too big and continually got bucked off. His continual meetings with the ground after an unsuccessful attempt to make the ride generally resulted in a few bruises and abrasions, maybe a few pulled muscles now and then, but no serious injuries.

I had done a considerable amount of rodeoing when I was younger and could see that Doug was too big to ride the bareback broncs—he didn't have the coordination. He was trying to muscle the horses rather than use balance to ride them.

I finally told him, "Doug, you're too big to be tryin' those barebacks. You don't have the coordination to do that. You're a better roper than a bronc rider an' you'd be better off to stick to ropin'. You'd make more money an' be saving a lot of money, not havin' to pay the bronc entry fees."

A year or two later, when Doug had quit trying to ride broncs and concentrated on team roping, I heard him telling some of his friends, "Yep, I stopped tryin' the rough stock. Stu was the only guy honest enough to tell me straight. Now that I'm only doin' ropin', I been makin' more trips to the pay window at the rodeos an' I ain't been wakin' up in the morning stiff an' sore."

I didn't need to have the same conversation with Jason. I think his being gored put an end to his bull riding aspirations. But he did need to improve his horsemanship skills. As big as he was, he really needed to learn how to get on his horse properly, rather than just climb up as best he could.

In my training sessions for all new hands and the returning hands, I always go over getting on a horse properly. If a feller puts his left foot in the stirrup, then springs up off his right foot into the saddle, he can get into the saddle without pulling it towards him.

If a feller continually pulls the saddle towards him rather than springing up into the saddle, it will start a saddle sore on the horse, and then we can't use him.

Jason's problem was that he had plenty of muscle and he tried to use it rather than balance and coordination to get on a horse. After a few training sessions, Jason was still struggling with getting on.

"More spring!" I would holler, "more bounce!"

Jason struggled with this, but it got a little easier each time. Even though he didn't have the getting on down perfectly, he still had to guide rides.

Every time he had to go out on a ride, I would softly say, "More spring, more bounce!"

On one ride, Jason was to accompany the ride as a second guide. We had all the tourists horseback and they had started out. All Jason had to do was get on his horse and follow the ride.

Dave, the boss on the outfit, told Jason, "Get on your horse, your ride's leaving!"

"Don't forget to spring," I said.

Jason hurriedly got to his horse, put a foot in the stirrup, sprung up and went plumb over the horse and saddle! He landed unceremoniously on the ground!

Dave had watched the whole affair and was down on one knee, laughing, and laughing hard.

Jason sat up. "Is that enough spring?"

"You kinda got the idea," I said, laughing, "But you sorta overdid it."

"Better get on your horse and catch up to your ride," Dave said. He was getting up and still laughing.

Jason got on his horse, muttering something about "more bounce" and some other uncomplimentary comments.

"Better not get off your horse," hollered Dave. "You'll just have to get back on! But the customers might enjoy the show! That's pretty good entertainment!"

Jason joined the ride without incident.

As the summer progressed, Jason got better. When the summer ended, he went back to Georgia. During the winter I got a few calls from some dude outfits scattered around the West and was pleased to give Jason very favorable job recommendations. He did get hired on a dude outfit down by Buena Vista, Colorado, the following summer.

I had the opportunity to visit with the management of that outfit and they informed me Jason did a good job and didn't fall off getting on his horse.

He needed a full-time, year-round position and got hired on a cattle outfit by Steamboat Springs, Colorado.

Despite his problems getting on, which he finally mastered, he decided to make a career out of horses, cattle, and dudes.

Maggot

I have a problem remembering people's names. I'm sure the reasons have to do with the fact that I'm getting older and I don't pay really close attention. Part of it may also be due to the fact that I'm becoming hard of hearing. Regardless of the reasons, it generally takes me a few days to get all the new hired help's names correct.

I'm often reminded of my dad. I'm the oldest of six kids and my dad would quite often have to holler out each one of us kids' names before he got to the one he wanted.

"Stu! Jeff! Dave! Jim! Judy! Scott!"

Dad would holler out everyone's name, just like calling the roll in school, then go back and select the person he wanted.

"David! Come here, I need to talk to you." Most of the time he would get it right.

Trying to learn everyone's name, I would quite often use the same technique and then stumble trying to put the right name with the right face. But after a time I would eventually get it right.

I had a particularly rough time with one new hand. All the hands were seated at the supper table when I showed up. I was a little late, having to handle some minor problem, and then having to get cleaned up.

As I entered the kitchen, she was introducing herself to the other hands and getting acquainted. I really didn't hear her clearly.

"What did you say your name was, Maggot?"

My question was met with a very hostile stare and silence.

"Well?" I still hadn't got an answer.

"I am called Magna." Her reply was very curt. She went on to explain that Magna was a nickname for something else and I quickly lost interest. I was getting more information than I needed or wanted and what I really wanted was supper!

I thought I could remember Magna easy enough. Magna is a town west of Salt Lake City, and my oldest daughter lives there. However, the name "Maggot" stuck with me, and I had to be careful when I ran down the roll like my dad. I was severely tempted to call her Maggot, but as she appeared to take exception to the name, I thought better of it. However, every time I called her Magna, my mind was thinking Maggot.

The next morning, Dave, the boss, took the crew out on a short ride to acquaint everyone with the various flowers, plants and trees. Generally, I don't go on these excursions, but I was told to go by Dave. I was to follow and give Dave a report as to everyone's riding level.

Our tourist rides in the park are all walking, but on these educational excursions we could move out a little faster and it was common to trot to get to a particular area to save time. On this particular trip, there was a lot more trotting than there had been on similar trips.

When we got back to the stable, Dave asked me, "Can that Magna ride?"

"Well," I said, "she does all right at a walk, but she's all over the saddle at a trot. She does seem to have some riding experience, but not a lot."

"She's from New York and probably did all her riding in Central Park. She's actually an opera singer," continued Dave.

"We'll see how she does," I said.

Maggot seemed to have an attitude that, "If you can do it, so can I," regardless of whether she had some previous experience or not. She didn't really fit in with the crew all that well, although she indicated that she had a lot of experience with horses. After a few days, she was causing more problems than was necessary.

I generally drive the feed truck when we feed. The corrals are quite rocky and if a person doesn't drive real easy, he's liable to bounce the people that are throwing the hay into the feed bunks off the truck. We certainly don't want to get someone hurt.

Magna thought she would like to drive the truck and she assured me she'd had experience with a stick shift. Against my better judgment, I let her drive. Her experience with a stick shift was limited and she almost bounced me off the truck. After a great many stalls and starts, we got the feeding done.

A few of the other hands had been watching the feeding operation and confided in me that they didn't want to be throwing off the hay when Maggot was driving. I let them know that Maggot's driving experience at our stables had come to an abrupt end.

The name Maggot had stuck with the hands, although none of them used it when she was present.

She told me she had worked for an outfit in Wyoming that I was familiar with. I knew the boss on this outfit and thought I might give her a call to find out a little more about our new employee.

I couldn't talk to my friend directly, but left a message on her phone, asking about Magna.

The next day after work, I had a message on my cell phone from my friend in Wyoming. The message didn't start with a hello. It was simple.

"My God, Stu! Get rid of her as fast as you can!"

That was all there was and I privately told Dave of my findings.

"I've been trying to find a way to let her go without firing her," said Dave. "She's really not suited for this kind of work. But I really kinda feel sorry for her."

I don't know how he did it, but Maggot left. I think Dave had a discussion with her and she left of her own accord.

Now Dave will tell you that Maggot was my girlfriend. This was not the case. I really didn't want anything to do with her and I wouldn't take her to a dogfight, even if I thought she could win. If the truth were known, Maggot had somewhat of a crush on Dave.

One night, during suppertime, the phone rang. Dave got up from the table and answered it.

Dave returned to the supper table with an amused, concerned look on his face.

Noticing this, I asked, "What was that about?"

"That was Magna."

"Really! What did she want?"

"She got a job around here and wanted to come over and watch television," said Dave.

"Did you tell her to get some popcorn an' soda pop an' come on over?"

"No," replied Dave.

"Dave, I think she's got a crush on you! What did you tell her?"

"I told her, 'No'."

"And what did she say?" I knew part of Maggot's problem was that she questioned everything.

"She asked, 'Why not?'"

"And what did you tell her?"

"I told her that I needed my quiet time," replied Dave.

"That's a good line," I said. "I'll remember to use it myself sometime. But you may have missed an opportunity to get some free popcorn an' snacks!"

"I'll survive," answered Dave.

Maggot continued to call, although her calls were less frequent. Occasionally, Dave would try to tease me by saying she was my girlfriend, but I brushed it off, generally to Dave's amusement.

One morning, after the first ride had left, Dave said, "Your girlfriend called last night."

"My girlfriend!?" I was a little shocked. I didn't have a girlfriend at the time and didn't know of any ex-girlfriends in the area. "Who is that?"

"I think you call her Maggot."

"She ain't my girlfriend!"

"But she keeps calling here. She must be looking for you!"

"She ain't callin" for me! She's callin' for you, Dave! She's got a crush on you! You should do something about that rather than stringin' the poor girl along."

"I think she's after you," said Dave.

"Nope," I said. "She's never called me wantin' to watch television!"

Dave seemed to be taken back by my comment and, strangely enough, he has never mentioned my supposed girlfriend again.

Vagabonds

Back when I owned my own ranch, I'd always had to work in town, just to keep the ranch going. I didn't mind it so much, but I didn't have any free time. The pressures of the job in town and trying to get things done on a timely basis on the ranch did create some problems.

I had to move some cows. I didn't have a big herd to move, just a few cows and calves that I'd kept close to the house to keep an eye on while they calved. I didn't think it was going to be a big job, but I was limited on time. I was also running short on feed.

But the cattle needed to be moved and I had decided that today was the day to do it.

I did have some help. My wife and her three kids by a previous marriage were going to help me. The kids were pretty young, but big enough to stand in the driveways and lanes of the neighbors and keep the cattle headed down the road. We only had a few miles to go and it was all on the road.

I left my job at the regular time and made a beeline to the ranch. I had given instructions that we would move the cattle when I got off work, but when I got home, nobody was there. No wife, no kids, nor my saddle horse or cattle were present. I had a pretty good idea where they were, and knowing that my wife didn't like waiting, I started down the road looking for them. It wasn't too far when I found them.

The wife was riding my saddle horse behind the cattle, keeping them moving. She was sending the kids ahead of the cattle to stand in the driveways and keep the cows on the road. Of course, the kids were running, and as they ran up alongside the cattle, it caused the cattle to start running. She had cows on the road, in the neighbor's driveways and even some in the neighbor's gardens. Some of the calves had started to show signs of getting tired because of the running and trying to keep up with their moms.

I caught up to the bunch and was kinda upset. The whole operation looked like a bunch of vagabonds going down the road. I got my saddle horse from my wife and put her in the truck with instructions to just follow the cattle, real slow, and keep other cars from speeding through the herd. I got on the horse and proceeded to get the wayward cattle out of gardens and back on the road.

The idea about putting the kids in the driveways was a good one, and I would ride back and fourth along the herd, picking up a youngster on my saddle horse, then depositing the youngster in a driveway ahead of the cattle.

I picked up one child and gave her a ride to the next driveway. As we moved ahead of the herd, she made the remark, "This sure is a lot easier than running! A cattle drive is kinda fun, but is this the way they did it in the old days?"

"Not exactly," I said.

I agreed with her, but I had to change the operation of the situation. My horse wasn't used to riding double. I sure didn't want to get me and one of the kids bucked off! And he was getting a little tired constantly going from the front to the rear.

I thought it might be easier if the wife picked up the kids and placed them ahead of the cattle in the driveways and I would just follow along on the horse, keeping the stragglers up. The wife could keep the cattle on one side of the road as she passed by them and I could slow the approaching traffic down.

It worked pretty good, although the wife was complaining about having to constantly turn around!

We finally made it to the new pasture and I got around the herd to hold them. I didn't want to just turn the cows loose. If they didn't have a chance to "mother up" (reconnect with their calves), they would go back to the last place the calf sucked and look for their calves there. I didn't need any help mothering up the cattle so I sent the wife and kids home. I finally had a chance to relax a little. As I reflected on the "cattle drive," I wondered how many cattle would have made it to market in the old days if the cowboys had to walk. I don't think many would have and there wouldn't have been many western movies made if the cowboys looked like vagabonds.

But the cattle got moved, they got mothered up, and I got to do the nightly chores when I got home.

Good News—Bad News

I try to have a little fun on our dude rides. For one thing, it's kinda hard to be a little nervous and scared when another person is laughing or smiling. That helps out our dudes. Another reason is that joking around helps to relieve the boredom.

I have been around our trails in Rocky Mountain National Park so many times, I could do them blindfolded. Besides that, my horse knows the trails, and other than watching that he doesn't take a shortcut home, riding him is like having auto-pilot or cruise control.

Sure, it's interesting to see wildlife and to note the minute changes in the scenery from day to day, but after a while, it all becomes commonplace. So, a little humor helps to relieve the monotony.

When I'm leading a ride, I'll generally have the kids aged six and older right behind me so I can keep an eye on them. It's a little difficult to start a conversation with these youngsters, but I try. I'll start by asking them their name. Sometimes they're so infatuated with watching their horse, they'll not answer me. When this happens, I'll ask them, "How old are you?"

The answer might come back, "Eight."

"Do you want to make it to nine?"

Sometimes I don't get an answer. Occasionally, the youngster will just shrug their shoulders, as if to say, "I don't know."

Most of the time the youngsters will answer, "Yes."

"If you want to make it to nine, then do what you're told!"

This exchange will generally bring a smile from the parents, usually trailing along right behind them. The kids will usually just look at me, not fully understanding the meaning and that I'm just joking with them.

The next question is, "What grade in school are you in?"

"Third," might be the answer.

"How do you like the third grade?"

"It's okay." Some of the kids aren't really too excited about school.

"You know," I'll continue, "I liked the third grade so much, I went for two years!"

Sometimes the kids will understand this—the parents always do—and it's good for a laugh.

After trying to joke with the kids, pointing out wildlife and certain geological features, our ride will be coming to an end. About two hundred yards from, and out of sight of, the stables, I'll stop the ride, move off the trail so I can see all the riders, then tell them, "Well folks, I got some good news an' some bad news for you. What do you want first?"

Generally the answer will be, "The bad."

"The bad news is, our ride is almost over!"

I'm sure that's not bad news for everyone. After two hours in the saddle, getting a little stiff and saddle sore, I'm sure that's good news for some of the folks. It might be real welcome, good news for some of them.

I'll continue with instructions as to what to do when we reach the stables.

"When we reach the stables, stay on your horse until one of the wranglers can come an' help you off your horse."

Then, I'll wait for the question.

"What's the good news?"

"The good news is very simple. We ain't lost no more!"

I'll lead the ride back to the stables, amidst a few chuckles.

Free Room and Board

When I had my rental horse stables in Grand County, Colorado, I was always looking to buy good, gentle horses to use in our dude string, along with some extra equipment. About the only time off I got was when I went to a horse sale.

I went to a horse sale in Parshall, Colorado, hoping to get a few more saddles and, more importantly, a few more good horses that I could use for the rental horse string.

I did get a few saddles, but horses were quite expensive that day and I didn't get any. There were a lot I would have liked to buy, but I just couldn't justify the price. I had figured a formula by which I could pay so much for a horse based on what I thought the horse would generate in income. The formula wasn't complicated, I just needed to figure out how much it would cost to feed the horse for a year, shoeing and vet bills, overhead, essentially all the costs for a year then subtract that from what I hoped the horse would make. I would get to keep the difference for me.

I bid on quite a few horses and even exceeded my limit once or twice, but couldn't get anything bought. I was getting a little discouraged. I was working the horses I had too hard and had hoped to get a few more horses to lighten the load on them. I needed horses we could ride for a day or two to see what we actually had, then go to renting them out.

One of the horse traders at the sale noticed that I hadn't bought anything and at the end of the sale he said, "Didn't get anything today, did you?"

"Nope," I answered.

"How many were you looking to get?"

"I figured I could use five or six, if the price was right," I said.

"Well," said the horse trader, "I've got some. I could bring them by, let you use them, and then you buy what you want. That would help me out as I'm starting to run short of feed."

"Lookin' for some free room an' board? That sounds pretty good to me, but what's your price? Theses horses were too expensive for me today." I was just joking about the free room and board.

"We can discuss price if there's anything you want when I come to get what you don't want."

"Are they shod?"

"They will be," answered the horse trader.

"We can do that," I said. "When do you want to bring 'em by?"

"I can get them to you next week!"

"That sounds good to me," I said. "I'll need a brand inspection an' we'll be in business."

"Yeah," said the horse trader. But he didn't sound quite as excited about the deal as when he first approached me. I wondered if he would show up with the horses.

A week went by and the horse trader didn't show up. I made plans to go to a horse sale over on the Front Range, outside Denver.

The horse trader never did show up, but the brand inspector did. He was an older feller and he knew what he was doing.

Very carefully, he looked over all the horses in my corrals, without going into the corrals. We visited on my office porch and he carefully looked over every horse that came in off a ride. When he was satisfied that he had seen every horse on the property, he said, "The reason for my visit is that there were five horses stolen from over by Kremmling a few weeks ago, and I thought you might have seen them."

Might have seen them, I thought. *What you're actually saying is, you thought I might have stole 'em!* However, I didn't say anything.

The brand inspector described the stolen horses by their colors, markings, and brands.

"I'll be glad to show you papers on all my horses. They're up at the house if you want to see 'em."

"That won't be necessary," replied the inspector. "I'm satisfied they aren't here."

I thought to myself, *I knew you thought I stole 'em!*

A few weeks later, a feller was arrested for horse stealing. The horses that were stolen from the Kremmling area were spotted in a pasture near Grand Junction, Colorado, and were traced to the individual that was arrested. That individual went to trial and was found guilty. He went to prison for two years. As it turned out, the feller that went to prison was the same horse trader that wanted me to try out some horses to see if I liked them well enough to buy them.

I thought he was looking to get some free room and board for his horses for a while and he ended up getting some free room and board for himself at the Colorado state pen for two years!

It occurred to me that if I had let him bring the horses to my place without a brand inspection, I could very well have been the guy that went to prison! Of course, the reason he didn't bring the horses is that he didn't dare get a brand inspection on them.

A Bargain Price

Keeping horses shod is pretty much a full time job. After all the horses are shod, there might be a couple of weeks when everything is good, but a horse generally needs his shoes reset about every six weeks. That's about the rate most horses' hooves grow. The horses that we use a lot might wear out their shoes in about three or four weeks, depending on how rocky the trails are.

Shoeing horses is a job I don't particularly like. It's hard, backbreaking work. If a feller has a lot of horses to keep shoes on, it's better to hire a professional farrier. Because most all of the horses were shod at about the same time to start with, they'll all need to be reshod at about the same time. That makes for a lot of work, and if I had to do it by myself, that's more work than I want and it would take me away from my other duties.

The timing can create a little bit of a problem. I'd rather have my dude horses out marching the trail, making money, than standing tied along the corral fence waiting for new shoes. It's real important to get the shoes on fast and properly.

One year I did hire a couple of horseshoers and they worked well together. I didn't quite understand the one feller. He kept telling me that he shod eleven or twelve horses every day. I knew that to be a little far-fetched. If a guy can shoe ten horses a day, that's a pretty good day's work. And that's if the horses will stand good.

However, I found out that he wasn't really shoeing eleven or twelve horses a day. Eleven or twelve was the number of shoes he was putting on each day! I thought that maybe I ought to tell him that a horse has four feet and that a shoe is required on each foot, but I didn't want to get involved in an intellectual discussion with a horseshoer. These guys can't be too smart—if they had any sense they'd be doing something else for a living!

Because of the rush of trying to get as many horses shod as fast as possible and still take out our guided tourist rides, we were not too particular about keeping the shoeing area real clean. The old shoes are pulled off the horses and just tossed aside, out of the way.

After all the horses have a new set of shoes, then we can clean up the area. The old shoes aren't worth anything and we used to take them to the dump. But some folks, particularly kids, wanted to have one for a souvenir, so we started gathering them up, putting them in a barrel, and selling them for a dollar apiece. We made some money doing that, but we'd generally give away as many as we'd sell. Sometimes it's hard to deny a cute little seven- or eight-year-old girl a souvenir of her horse-riding experience in Colorado.

One day, when the farriers had finished and left, I had the wranglers that weren't out on rides clean up the shoeing area.

"Gather up all them old shoes an' put 'em in the barrel," I said. "We can sell 'em for a dollar a piece as souvenirs during the summer."

The crew got started and I heard a strange question. "What do you want to do with these shoes that are broken in half?"

A lot of horses will wear out the toes on the front shoes and the shoe will break. The wrangler that had asked the question

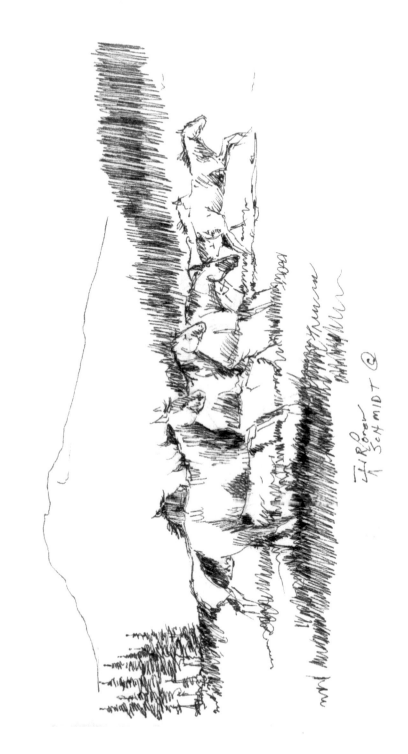

was standing in the middle of the shoeing area with a befuddled look on his face, holding up one of these half shoes.

I turned and surveyed the situation. The half shoe certainly wasn't worth anything. Being somewhat awestruck at the absurdity of the question, I answered simply, "Toss it in the barrel. We'll sell it for fifty cents!"

It was tossed in the barrel.

I don't think it ever sold.

Too Much to Eat

As a teenager, I got a job on a fairly large-size cattle ranch in Utah. I thought I would be doing a lot of cattle work, riding a lot of horses, doing a lot of roping and riding, doing those things that cowboys do. After all, I'd had a lot of experience working closer to home for neighbors.

I was disappointed. I spent a lot of time irrigating and doing odd jobs. I was just a ranch hand, not a cowboy. I was told we had to move a big herd of sheep to a new range and it would take five or six days. I looked forward to it. Five or six days following a herd of sheep horseback would be a lot better than five or six days irrigating. I was pretty sure I wouldn't be taking any wild rides through the brush with my rope swinging, chasing an outlaw sheep trying to make an escape, but I figured being horseback would be a lot better than being afoot doing odd jobs.

But I was sorely disappointed. We were going to be afoot trailing the sheep! This was not a job for the cowboy I thought I was!

But, I had a job and had to do it. I don't know how many miles I walked, but I do know I walked, and even ran, more miles than any one of them sheep. I was footsore—I hadn't brought any shoes along, all I had were cowboy boots, and it's hard to walk long distances in cowboy boots on any kind of ground.

We finally got the sheep where they belonged and I was glad to be done with them. I was tired, footsore, and my shoulder ached. I had taken to throwing rocks or whatever I could at the sheep that were straying too far from the herd, rather than getting around them and herding them back into the herd. I never have been a good thrower; however, I got a lot better on that trail drive.

My spirits picked up considerably when I was told I would be going up by the cow camp and doing some odd jobs in that area. I thought I might get horseback and maybe improve my roping. The thought of roping with my sore shoulder wasn't pleasant, but the thought of roping something rather than throwing rocks at sheep improved my state of mind.

I was told to get my stuff and was taken to a camp about a mile from the cow camp. My job was to help another ranch hand cut aspen trees and build a fence. We would need a lot of trees—the fence would be all aspen logs, notched at each end, and placed on top of each other at right angles all the way around a twenty-acre parcel.

I wasn't too good with an axe, but I did cut almost as many trees down as the guy I was helping. We'd trim off the branches so we could get right to work building fence. There was a work-horse in the pasture where the cowboys kept their horses and I'd have to catch him in the morning, harness him, and ride him back to our camp so we could use him to snake the trees to where we were building fence. Then at night I'd have to take him back to the cow camp, take the harness off, and turn him loose.

I got tired of walking the horse back and forth to camp, so I started riding him. That sure beat walking, and with the harness on him, he was real easy to get on.

Everyone got Sunday off, and I used to go to the cow camp to visit with the cowboys. Actually, I was hoping they'd take a liking to me and want me to help them with the cows. That never happened. However, they did feed me.

One Sunday they had a big feed, and I probably ate more than my share. When it came time to leave, one of the cowboys suggested I catch a horse and ride him back to my camp.

I liked the idea, but I said, "I don't have a bridle."

"Catch that old gray horse. He's gentle an' you can ride him with a piece of binder twine," came the reply.

I hunted up a piece of binder twine, caught up the gray horse and proceeded to fashion a loop in the twine. I put the loop in the horse's mouth and had enough left to make one rein. I figured I could direct rein the horse to the left and neck rein the horse to the right. I thought this was the old Indian way of riding and although I hadn't done it before, I figured I'd be all right.

Things went all right as we started out. I turned the horse in both directions and he seemed to respond reasonably well enough, to start out. But the horse didn't stop well.

We headed toward my camp and got in a little bit of a rush. The horse had started out in an easy lope, but quickly picked up speed. I tried to slow him down some, but he wasn't responding. I was doing a good job of riding him until he went left around a bush and I went right.

I hit the ground and rolled up against another bush like a bowling ball about to make a strike. I wasn't hurt, just kind of dusty. I got up, brushed as much of the dust off as I could, and started to walk to my camp.

I hadn't walked ten yards before I started to get a funny feeling in the pit of my stomach. Walking another ten yards, I started to feel my supper coming up. Another ten yards and I doubled over and deposited my supper in the sagebrush!

I was embarrassed even though there was no one around to see. I decided that getting back to camp after a big meal might be better done on foot!

Modern Gadgets

Years ago, when I was a teenager, I saw what I thought was a pretty slick innovation. In the saddlery and harness section of Sears and Roebucks there was a specially made saddle labeled "Sheepherder Special." In the swells of the saddle was a transistor radio. The tree had been cut out so a small portable transistor radio could be inserted.

I could imagine an old sheepherder out on the desert listening to the latest news or his favorite music station. I remember thinking, *What's the world coming to? All the modern convinces of living in town out on the desert. It won't be long before they're putting television sets in saddles. I wonder how they'll insert the antenna.*

At the horse stables a couple of years ago, I got on a horse and went out to monitor how a ride was going. While I had to stay on the established trails set by the Park Service, I did manage to take a few shortcuts and end up ahead of the ride.

I was surprised to see the guide riding along, holding something in his hand and concentrating heavily on what he was doing. He wasn't watching his riders at all.

"What are you doing?"

The guide was totally surprised by my question. He was so involved in what was in his hand that he hadn't even seen me.

"I got a text message on my phone and was sending them an answer."

His reply didn't sit well with me. During our training sessions, I had repeatedly stressed the fact that we weren't in the horse business, we were actually in the people business. If the truth were known, we were actually babysitters for the adults on our guided trail rides.

"What did the message say?"

"It was a response to a job application I sent, for a job when I'm done here."

Looking for a job while he was on the job for me didn't sit well with me. I wanted all his attention on what he was doing for me, guiding inexperienced riders on horseback rides in Rocky Mountain National Park.

"You need to put that away and pay attention to your job here, while you still have a job here!"

I was totally displeased, but couldn't give him the cussing out I wanted to because there were tourists on the ride, and I really don't believe in disciplining my help in front of the customers.

"You an' I will have a little discussion when we get back to the stables."

I followed the ride in, just to make sure the guide was doing what he should for the rest of the ride.

At one time I had a little one-man stable at Silvercreek, Colorado. Not having anyone to watch the office and listen for the phone, I got a cell phone. I kept it with me all the time so I could keep somewhat of a handle on the business, even when I was out guiding rides. I had a selection of ring tones and selected the William Tell Overture as my ringer. That was the theme song for *The Lone Ranger* television program.

I didn't get many calls, but when I did get one out on a ride, the tourists thought it was amusing. One little kid even asked me, "Are you actually the Lone Ranger?"

Taken back, I answered, "Yes."

"Where's your mask?"

"I'm in disguise," I replied

Lately though, I have noticed a big surge in technological innovation. Some of my help have showed up with strange devices in their ears. I was beginning to think there was a large increase in people with hearing problems. I would ask them, "Are you hard of hearing?"

"No," would be the reply.

"What's that in your ear?"

"It's an iPod."

"What's an iPod?

"You can listen to music with it. It makes the day go a little better."

I suppose that's all right, but I would rather have the help trying to make the operation as a whole a little better than listening to pop music.

Recently, I watched a wrangler studying his cell phone intently.

"What are you doing?"

"I'm playing solitaire," was the reply.

Things have certainly changed since I saw the "Sheepherder Special" in the Sears store. I'm not sure all the change is for the good.

An Excellent Report

I'm always interested in how people got along on their horseback rides, so I generally ask them. Of course, some people I don't have to ask, I can tell by the way they walk when they get off their horse.

With these folks, when I see them walking, or hobbling away, I generally have a comment like, "What are you doing, trying to impersonate the way I walk?"

To some of the people, if I've got them sized up to take some good-natured joking, I'll ask, "Don't you know it's impolite to make fun of a crippled-up old cowboy like me?"

We'll most always have a good laugh about how stiff they are when they're done riding, and frequently I'll hear the comment, "Two hours was a little much for me, but it was really beautiful and worthwhile!"

I'll respond, "I arranged it that way especially for you."

"You did a good job!"

I really wonder if these folks realize I didn't really arrange it, although trail selection is very important in showing the country at its best.

Some folks don't feel as stiff as others when they're done, and to these folks, I'll ask, "How did you get along?" The answer is almost always positive.

There always seems to be a few moments of relief at the end of a ride. I don't know if the people are relieved that they made it back safe and sound, or just overjoyed that it's over!

Regarding quite a few of the horses, I'll ask, "How did your horse treat you?"

Once again, the answer is almost always positive, but I know the horses pretty good. It's important to ask the right question with the right people and the right horses. If I don't use some good judgment here, I could open a can of worms.

I was particularly interested in one young girl and how she got along on the trail ride. She was only eleven or twelve and had never rode before. She seemed very apprehensive before the ride and was quite scared. I picked a special horse for her and figured she'd be scared for the first ten or fifteen minutes of the ride, then she'd begin to relax, like most folks, and enjoy the ride.

When the ride got in, I took great pains to help her off her horse. She was very relaxed and had a big smile on her face. She looked like she had a good time.

"How did you do?"

"Fantastic!" Her reply was enthusiastic.

"Fantastic! How do you know?"

"I didn't fall off my horse," she replied, "and I didn't wet my pants!"

The other folks on the ride heard her answer and had a good laugh. I had a good laugh also. I have never before or since got an answer like that!

New Help, New Equipment

Over the years we've not had much luck hiring people after the beginning of the season. I hired two people that worked out extremely well. Josie was one and Bethany was the other. Both girls we would rehire, not just because we knew what we were getting, but because they did their work extremely well and surpassed our expectations.

We had some misgivings about Josie. She had her hair dyed in streaks. Her streaked hair earned her the nickname "Skunky." The nickname didn't stick, probably because she was first-class help. The guy that gave her the nickname continued to use it, but after helping us out for a couple of days, we could tell she knew what she was doing. We would have liked to have had her back every year, but as she had found a permanent, year-round job, I advised her to stick with her position, as we only hired part-time for the summer.

Bethany was altogether different. She had a good work ethic, knew something about a horse, and didn't have streaks in her hair. Whereas Josie was somewhat forward and outgoing, Bethany was kind of quiet and reserved. Josie mixed well with the other hands, but Bethany was a little slow fitting in. However, that changed.

Bethany was on vacation with her family in Colorado and went for a horseback ride with us. I noticed her and her family hanging around after their ride, but didn't pay much attention— I was busy getting another ride out.

When the ride departed, Dave, the boss, came to me.

"There's a good-looking young lady that wants to talk to you about a job."

"You know I've always got time to talk to the good-looking young ladies," I replied. "Where is she?"

I knew where she was, with her parents, and answered Dave loud enough so she and her family could hear.

"She's right over there," Dave said, pointing to where the family was standing, grinning, obviously pleased with my remark.

"You girls form a line an' I'll talk to each one of you privately," I said, as I walked over to them. I have always operated under the delusion that I am somewhat of a ladies man.

They grinned as I approached.

"How can I help you?"

"We would like to talk to you about a job."

"All of you want to work here?"

The family consisted of Bethany, her sister, and her parents.

"No, no. Just Bethany. She's had some experience with horses and needs a summer job." Bethany's mother was doing the talking.

"What are you trying to do, pawn off a troubled teenager on me for the summer?"

The family laughed at this comment.

"What are your qualifications? What do you want to do? You know, this isn't all just ridin' around Rocky Mountain National Park horseback. Quite often there's some pretty hard, distasteful work involved."

I decided to cut down on the humorous approach and pay attention to business.

We visited for a while, with Bethany's mom doing most of the talking. I found out that the vacation was going to be another week and a few days longer.

I wasn't totally convinced Bethany was going to work out, but I was willing to give her a try. Besides that, it was still early in the year and some of our help was already quitting.

"I'll tell you what I'll do. We'll try you out for a week. If, at the end of the week you work out, we'll give you a job 'till the first of October. If you stay 'till we agree, they'll be an end of the season bonus for you. If you don't work out, we'll give you a hundred bucks for a week's work, plus room and board, and say that at least we tried."

This deal was acceptable to everyone and Bethany put her stuff in the bunkhouse.

Bethany's work was more than adequate and at the end of the week, she was hired on. She asked for a day off to go shopping and was given it. Her folks took her to town and bought her the basics for what she needed to work—boots, jeans, and a new hat. Her folks even bought her a new headstall. She had the basics.

Coming to work off her vacation, she didn't have all her horse equipment. During the summer she started to acquire more horse and cowboy furnishings.

After a day off, Bethany showed up to work with a new pair of spurs. I don't remember if she had brought her chaps or if her parents had sent them later, but she had a pair of shotgun chaps. They were a little warm for the hot summer days. They were kinda cute, they had fringe going all the way around the back of the belt. I'd never seen something like that.

It wasn't too much later when, after a day off, she showed up to work with a new pair of chinks. The chinks were certainly more practical and they were cooler. Bethany's chinks were kinda fancy; they had been tanned with the hair still on. They were off a Herford critter and they really looked good, the red and white hair made a striking contrast.

I figured these chaps were made more for the show ring than for riding out in the open. I'd shy away from a pair of these chaps; I don't even know what kind of oil a feller would use to keep them in shape.

The end of the season was approaching and the weather was turning cooler. Most of the hired help had already departed to go back to college. Bethany, Evan, and I were the only hired help left.

We were sitting in the barn, waiting for the day to warm up. It was cool enough, I had already put my long johns on and Bethany had her new chinks on for warmth. Bethany made a joke or something and I reached over and slapped her on the knee.

"That's a good one!" I said. As I slapped her on the knee I felt the hair on her chaps. "My goodness! You have hairy legs!"

This brought another laugh from Bethany and Evan.

Then, Evan pulled out his pocketknife.

"Here," he said, as he handed the knife to Bethany, "Do you want to shave?"

We had a little fun that year, and Bethany worked out better than my expectations. I wish we could find more help like her every year.

R·LOREN
SCHMIDT

A Good Seat

Nelson and I worked together for four years guiding tourist rides near Jackson, Wyoming. His brother owned the outfit and Nelson was more or less the barn boss. I seemed to get along with Nelson pretty good, although a lot of folks found him difficult to work with. He was pretty well set in his ways; he had a way of doing things, and his way was right, at least on that outfit.

Nelson didn't own much. He had his horse, Poker, his dog, Bandit, his truck, and his saddle.

I admired his horse. He was a pull back, meaning that if he was tied to a rail, at some point he'd back up and keep backing until something gave or busted. He had the run of the place because he couldn't be tied. The horses were tied in the barn all day, and they had feed in front of them. They were watered at least twice a day and before they went out on a ride. But Poker was built pretty good and he was pretty well trained. He'd back up and side pass on cue, and he neck reined, which is about all the special talents a guide horse on a dude outfit needs to do.

I'd seen Nelson use the horse and admired the way Poker responded when asked to ease up beside another horse so Nelson could adjust a lead rope or whatever without getting off. If Poker didn't respond correctly to a cue, Nelson would reprimand him, sometimes harshly, but I think that's why Poker was such a good horse. He'd learned, perhaps the hard way, to respond correctly.

The dog, Bandit, I just tolerated. I don't have much use for dogs on a dude outfit. Bandit used to just follow along on Nelson's rides but the second year I worked for them, she quit doing that. She was getting old.

Nelson's saddle was something. It was a McCall, built on a Wade tree. There was something different about it, but I couldn't put my finger on it. I didn't know just what it was.

Nelson was a perfectionist, perhaps that's why so many people had a tough time getting along with him.

I asked him one time, after a ride with some particularly difficult tourists, "How are you getting' along with all these tourists?" I knew he'd had a tough time on the ride, I'd been with him, and he had become quite frustrated.

"That was a tough go," he replied. "I don't think I've ever heard so many dumb, stupid questions on one ride in my whole life."

"Well," I said, "You have to remember that these tourists are out of their element. I suppose, if you or me were in their environment, we'd be just as lost. And, of course, in this business, sometimes the hired help ain't much better than the tourists."

My last comment was directed at Nelson. He'd been having some trouble with some of the hired help and they'd been having some difficulty with him. I didn't want any of the help to get frustrated and quit. We needed everyone we had to help get the horses saddled every morning.

"That might be right," answered Nelson. "But with regard to some of the dumb, stupid things the tourists do, an' sometimes the hired help, I think its plumb disgusting! You just think it's funny."

"Well, it is," I said.

But Nelson was a perfectionist—in everything. He was in charge of keeping the saddles in tiptop shape, and he did this exceptionally well. Any little adjustment that had to be made to a saddle or its parts was made on the spot, and made to be a permanent repair, rather than a temporary fix. He would have been an excellent saddlemaker had he decided to go that direction.

I still couldn't figure out what was different about Nelson's saddle. It looked pretty much like other McCall saddles built on a Wade tree, but there was something different about it that I couldn't put my finger on.

One spring, before we started doing one- and two-hour rides, Nelson and I were oiling saddles and making minor repairs to equipment. We were using olive oil rather than neatsfoot oil because the olive oil didn't darken the leather like the neatsfoot.

As we were working, I took the opportunity to ask Nelson, "What is it about your saddle that makes it different than the other Wades on the outfit? There's something different an' I've racked my brain tryin' to figure out what it is, an' still don't know."

"I peeled back the leather over the seat and put a piece of beveled leather, starting at next to nothing up to about a quarter inch up toward the gullet. That gives the seat just a little more dish and, at least for me, it makes it more comfortable. You noticed that quarter-inch difference in the seat?"

"I didn't notice the quarter inch, but I noticed something different," I said.

Later that summer, in between rides, when we were just sitting around loafing and waiting for the next ride, Poker came wandering up to the barn where we saddled, probably looking for some extra grain. Nelson caught him, tightened the cinch, and said to me, "Come here."

That was Nelson's way, gruff, somewhat demanding, short and to the point.

"Here, get on this horse an' see what you think of him."

I got on the horse and settled in the saddle. I moved the horse in a little circle away from the barn and just sat there.

"Put the horse through his paces," said Nelson. "See what he can do!"

"I know what the horse can do," I said. "I've watched you an' him for the last couple of years! What I really wanted was to sit in this saddle an' see if it's as comfortable as it looks!"

I could have asked Nelson if I could sit in his saddle, but I always thought that would be a breach of western custom. It was better that Nelson invited me to sit on his horse, in his saddle. I think Nelson was a little disappointed in me that I didn't put Poker through his paces, but I was perfectly satisfied.

The saddle was as comfortable as it looked and today I ride a McCall, built on a Wade tree.

Soaring With Turkeys

It's hard to get lost on our trails. They're well signed and the horses have marked them well. Occasionally, hikers will take a wrong trail and when we meet them with our trail rides, we're always happy to help them get straightened out.

When I meet hikers on the trail, I'll generally ask them to step aside for the horses and continue, "Do you know where you are?"

It's important we ask them to move aside for the horses, as we don't know exactly how some of the horses will react to the backpacks and other paraphernalia they carry. We don't want someone falling off because their horse was spooked by a hiker.

The answer most often is, "Yes."

Then I'll ask, "Do you know where you're going?"

Once again the answer is, "Yes"

"Well, that's good! Can you tell us where we are an' where we're goin'?"

This remark is generally good for at least a smile from the hikers and a laugh from our riders. Most of the time these encounters are uneventful, although sometimes the hikers don't see the safety aspect involved in having them move off the trail.

While its difficult to get lost on the trails, quite often, early in the season when the help is still new, the trail guides do get confused.

Such was the case with Paige. We only had a few horses in the corral and they were saddled, ready to go to work. We had a few customers show up, wanting to go for a ride. I needed to show Paige the trail, but didn't want to leave the office unattended. With paying customers, I could justify putting a sign on the office door that said we would return at such and such a time, and take our riders out and show Paige the trail at the same time.

I formulated the plan, got the money, got the dudes on their horses and started out on our first guided ride of the season.

The trail hadn't changed during the winter. Maybe some of the ruts were a little deeper due to the spring runoff, but the scenery hadn't changed. Long's Peak was still in the same place and a few of the trees had been blown over, but it was still the same.

I was careful to point out to Paige various landmarks that might be helpful in timing her rides in the future. The ride went without incident and, as I recall, we even made a tip when it was over.

After the dudes left, I pointed out a few things to Paige about the trail then asked her if she felt comfortable with the trail.

"Can you take out a ride by yourself an' not get lost?"

Paige assured me she could.

"That's good," I said. "There's another girl supposed to show up tonight, an' tomorrow you can show her the trail if we have any business."

Once again Paige assured me she could handle the situation.

The next day, we did have some customers and Paige, along with the new girl, took the ride. I made a mental note of the time when they left.

We're actually selling timed horseback rides. If a guide shows up five or ten minutes late, it's all right. But if they come back fifteen minutes early, we're actually cheating our customers, and this is unacceptable.

Paige's first guided ride was more than fifteen minutes late coming in and I was getting concerned. I was catching up a horse to go out and look for her and her riders when I saw them coming through the trees and down the hill.

We got the riders off and they all told me it was a good ride and they all had a good time. I was relieved that there hadn't been an accident and no one was hurt.

When the riders left, I asked Paige, "What happened?"

"I got turned around on the trail," she answered.

"More like lost." It was the new girl.

"How did you get lost?"

"She went right instead of left." The new girl was being most helpful.

"I got on the wrong trail," answered Paige.

"Where?"

"I don't know."

"There's really only three places where you can make a wrong turn on the trail, which one was it?" I was getting somewhat upset. I had just showed her the trail the day before.

"I'm not sure," answered Paige.

"It was where the sign said, UP HILL HORSE TRAFFIC ONLY." The new girl seemed to know more about the trail than Paige.

"You went right instead of left at the sign? I guess I'll have to go over the trail with you again," I said.

I stopped my inquiry of Paige. She was quite embarrassed and it was clear to me she had got lost or turned around on the trail. I had some misgivings about how the summer was going to go, we had a long way to go. I left thinking, *It's hard to soar with the eagles when you have to work with the turkeys.* I even wondered if I would have to "soar with the turkeys" this year!

Lightning Rod

Sometimes it's hard to figure out the capabilities of our new help. They arrive with various levels of experience and skill. Such was the case with Michael.

His experience with horses was limited to say the least, and although he was willing to do anything, his abilities were somewhat limited. I was a little concerned as to just how I was going to use him at the rental horse stable and still get our money's worth out of him. He did get along well with the general public and I think he knew everything about every video game invented.

Because of his limited ability with horses, I had pretty well resigned myself to using Michael as a second guide, always sending a more experienced guide with him. He fulfilled this role well, but because of his inexperience, he ended up being a chore boy quite a lot of the time. I think this was his first time away from home.

Michael's family was coming out for a ride and Michael was quite excited about taking them out on the trail, guiding his first ride unassisted.

I heard about this and questioned the boss, Dave, about the wisdom in letting Michael guide this ride.

"How safe do you think this will be?"

"He should be all right. Just put his family on the good, old dependable horses," answered Dave.

"I'm not sure about the liability of this," I said.

"It will be all right. If something does happen, Michael's family certainly won't sue us because he's incompetent!"

The plan was made and I decided to have a little fun with the family when they showed up. I do have a little leeway running the office and quite often use it.

Michael's family showed up and he was there to introduce me to them. His mother, sister, an uncle, along with a few family friends, were present.

It's normally our custom to give a little discount to immediate family members of our hired help and I was prepared to give the discount, but have some fun first.

"Generally, we give a discount to immediate family members for a horse ride," I said. "And because Michael is working for us, we should give you a discount. However, because we haven't got the work out of Michael that we expected, I've been instructed to charge you folks double!"

Michael's sister and uncle, and the family friends laughed at this statement, but Michael's mother looked a little frustrated. However, she started fumbling in her purse and asked, "How much will it be?"

She actually believed me and took me seriously!

"Lady, I'm just joking with you," I said. "We can give you and your daughter a discount, but everyone else will have to pay the full price."

Michael's mother looked very relieved and paid for everyone. I guess she knew more about her son than we did!

The ride went well and without incident. Michael's mother, although somewhat taken back with my humor, came in very relaxed and even joked with me some before they left.

R. LOREN
SCHMIDT @.

On another occasion, Michael was sent as a second guide on a ride. The ride went well, although a fierce thunderstorm had developed after they left. Everyone came in with their raincoats on, but still relatively dry.

Strangely, Michael came in standing up in the saddle.

When the riders were leaving their raincoats at the office, I asked Michael, "Why were you standin' up in the saddle when you came in? You gettin' saddle sore?"

"No," replied Michael.

One of the guests heard the question, and replied, "We convinced him to stand up in the saddle when the lightning started up on the ridge and he obliged!"

"You were standin' in the saddle during a rainstorm?"

"Yes," replied Michael.

"What for?" I was becoming somewhat perplexed.

"We convinced him that he would be doing a great service for us if he stood up to attract the lightning," replied the guest.

"You mean you had him acting as a lightning rod?"

"Yes," answered the guest. "We even gave him a new nickname—Lightning Rod!"

Bear Scares

Bears can be a problem, especially around horses. Bears are predators and horses can be the prey. So there seems to be a built-in defense in horses when bears are around. A horse's defense is generally to run, to get as far away as possible from the bear and as quickly as possible.

At my stables in Grand County, Colorado, we didn't experience too many problems with bears. The horses did break out of the corrals one night, and that was attributed to a bear being in the area, but I couldn't find any tracks. I still don't know the exact reason why they broke out.

We had some Shetland ponies and a couple of miniature horses that we used for parents to lead their kids around on when the kids were too young or too small to handle their own horse on the trail. The kids had to be six or over to go on a trail ride and we didn't allow any double riding. We charged five dollars for a parent to lead the pony and youngster around for half an hour. The fee was half of the one-hour ride rate and the ponies more than paid their way.

On one occasion, I rented two ponies to some foreign tourists. They spoke broken English and I'm not sure where they

were from. They dressed in their native attire, long flowing robes, and some kind of scarves over their heads. I guessed they were from India, Pakistan, or somewhere in the Middle East; I really didn't know.

But they had American money and wanted to take their kids for a horseback ride. That's the business I'm in, so I took their money, caught up two ponies, helped put the kids on, told them where to go on the trail and sent them on their way with the admonishment, "Don't let the horses eat! If you let them eat they'll spend all your time eating and the kids won't get much of a ride. You have half an hour."

The procession left and I glanced at my watch, making a mental note of what time to expect them back, and I went back to the office to sell the longer rides. My help was already catching up horses and tying them to the rail to get the ride out. I didn't pay much attention, but the first horses to be brought out seemed a little nervous.

We had fifteen or sixteen riders on that ride and when they were all horseback, we gave them instructions on how to handle their horses and got ready to leave. Because of the number of riders, I had to send at least two guides on the ride to act as outriders.

The horses at the far end of the rail, the ones that were brought out first, were still acting nervous and the lead guide couldn't get her horse to leave the barn area.

I couldn't figure out why the horses were acting the way they were until I looked down the trail and saw the reason.

The foreigners were on the trail, just poking along. From the rail they looked just like a couple of large bears grazing! Their flowing robes and dark head scarves disguised their appearance!

On another occasion, I was driving a sleigh ride team northwest of Jackson, Wyoming, located on one of the buttes overlooking Jackson. I didn't much care for my team, as they weren't well matched; one was a bay horse that was hard to bridle because he had warts in his ears. I had to undo the cheekpiece, put the bit in his mouth, then buckle up the cheekpiece.

The other horse was a bottle-raised horse that was raised by the owner's wife. As a colt, the horse had full run of the place and quite often was in the way. Because he'd had his run of the place and been bottle-raised, his ground manners weren't very good.

But both horses worked well together and whether or not I liked them, I was stuck with them.

We had a sleigh ride one night that needed two sleighs. The boss would drive the first sleigh and I would follow in the second with my mismatched team. I would also have the boss's wife's granddaughter riding with me.

We started out and I expected a fairly routine ride, and it was, the first quarter of a mile from the stable. At the point where we crossed the road, which had been left unplowed of snow for our sleigh ride, a tourist in a SUV vehicle had driven off the regular road and onto our sleigh ride trail, slid off our sleigh ride trail and got stuck.

The boss and his sleigh made it past the stuck vehicle without a problem, but when my team started by, we had some trouble.

Big John, the bottle-raised horse, was eyeing the SUV suspiciously and edging toward the other horse. Anything out of place or anything new on the trail can spook a horse, and Big John appeared to be getting ready to spook. I was trying to talk soothingly and reassuringly to the horses to avoid trouble.

Just as we passed the stuck SUV, the driver of the vehicle crawled out from under the SUV, dragging a blanket. Apparently the driver had been trying to stuff the blanket under the tires in an effort to gain some traction to get out from his situation.

Big John saw the man crawling out from under the SUV. He looked just like a bear coming out of his winter den. Big John reacted immediately, and started to run as fast as he could. The other horse, not wanting to be out done and having to keep up because they were harnessed to the same sleigh, started running, too. We were having a runaway!

"Hold on!" I didn't want any of my passengers to get scared and jump off. "We're goin' to catch up to the other sleigh!"

The other sleigh was about a hundred and fifty yards ahead of us and I had to get the team slowed down before we crashed into them.

I tried to slow the team down, but without success. I tried to turn them into the deep snow to slow them down, but again without success.

The horses were slowing down some, but not because of anything I was doing. They were getting tired.

We did slow down before we hit the other sleigh. The granddaughter was sitting beside me.

"Are you folks all right?" I asked.

Affirmative replies came from the passengers.

"I was scared," said the granddaughter.

"So was I," I whispered back.

Bankers Versus Beekeepers

Tips in the horse rental business are fairly common, although a guide won't be able to retire on what he or she makes during the summer. A lot of folks just can't afford to shell out extra cash after paying for a family of say, five, to go on a two-hour ride at fifty bucks a horse for the ride.

I'm always careful to tell the guides to send their paychecks home or deposit them right in the bank, and use their tips, if they get any, to live on. A lot of folks tip a waitress fairly regularly, but are unaware that it's perfectly acceptable to tip a horse wrangler or guide for a ride. But, tips can't be counted on as a regular source of income.

I remember one time I was tipped in a most unusual manner. I had led a ride out and it was a good ride. It was a safe ride and everyone had a good time, we even saw some wildlife in the form of a few bull elk, in the velvet.

Even though it had been a good ride, I didn't get a monetary tip. But one of the riders went to his car then returned.

"We really had a good time," he said. "We wanted to give you something, but don't really have a lot of money, so we wanted to give you this."

He handed me a gift, wrapped in a brown paper sack. I noticed it was quite heavy for being no larger than it was. "This is the business we're in back home," he said.

I took the gift and set it aside, as I had other business to tend to. I thanked him and went back to work. I forgot all about the gift until closing time when I noticed it on the shelf where I had put it.

Opening it up, I really wasn't surprised to find a bottle of honey. I thought to myself, *I'll take this to the kitchen an' let all the hired help enjoy this.*

"This is what I made in tips today," I said, as I put the bottle of honey on the table. "You all can enjoy this."

One of the hands said, "If you made a buck, would you put it on the table for everyone to enjoy?"

Another said, "You need to start taking out more bankers than beekeepers! You'd be better off for it!"

"Bankers generally don't tip! They know how to hold onto their money. That's why they're bankers," I said.

As I recall, it was really good honey and it didn't sit on the kitchen table very long.

Evesdropping

Various conversations are always going on in the saddling room in the morning when we're getting the horses ready for the day's work. As the older hands, Dave and I generally don't pay much attention to this chitchat; we're watching what we're doing and watching that the other help does their job properly. We're also checking the horses to see who might be lame, who might be off a little, who might be missing a shoe, or who might have a saddle or cinch sore.

Dave and I don't really keep up with the talk and quite often if we hear something, we'll have to ask a question, then get filled in with regards to what they're talking about. We're not really interested in the night life around Estes Park, Colorado, or what the kids did the night before. Our main focus is to get the horses ready.

Sometimes the conversations are directed toward the horses in the form of a question, such as, "How are you doing this morning, Leopard?"

I've got into the habit of talking to the horses as I'm throwing saddles, and have done this all my life. I've never had an answer to my questions from the horse.

Reno is a bay mare that we've had for years. She's always worked well for us, but she's one of those horses that I haven't been able to trust completely, although she's never done anything wrong. She does have a little bit of an attitude, which gets a little worse as the summer wears on.

Reno came into the saddling chute one morning and was acting a little strange.

Ashley noticed Reno's strange behavior and asked Reno, "Are you in heat?"

Of course the horse didn't answer, but Dave, only hearing part of the talk, asked Ashley what she was talking about.

"I was asking Reno if she was in heat," replied Ashley.

"Oh," Dave said. "I thought you were asking Emily if she was in heat!"

Too Greedy?

Tristan was a big feller, big enough to be a football player. He had some previous riding experience, although he was too big to be a good bronc rider. Finding a horse for him to ride wouldn't be a problem; a lot of horses had been bought during the winter and a lot of big, work horse crosses had been purchased.

It's my habit to send an adequate number of guides on each ride. In the spring when we're trying out new horses and we really don't know how good our new hands are going to be, I send out more guides than are needed. The extra guides can watch the new horses and each other until we know what we have with horses and help.

Of course we don't send any tourists out on the new horses until we know the horses pretty well. Some of the new horses might never be suitable to be rented out and we'll use them for guide horses.

Tristan was always willing to accompany the rides when needed early in the year. But as the year went on and we got to know the horses and the help, we didn't need as many extra guides on each ride.

Tristan liked this. He had a real gift of gab, actually I thought he talked too much, consequently he did quite well in making tips from the tourists as I could send him out alone with five or six riders.

When Dave, the boss, came back from a horse sale with four or five new horses, I felt it was necessary to send extra guides on each ride that a new horse was used on. Tristan objected.

"Why send extra people? I can handle this ride by myself," he said. "Besides, I'm up for this ride."

I think Tristan had figured it out that extra guides would mean less tips as everyone on a ride was expected to split any tips received equally with the other guides. His major in college was finance.

"You're ridin' a new horse," I said. "An' I want to know what the horse does. The extra guides can help you with the tourists if you need it, an' they can tell me what your horse is like. This ain't no different than it was earlier in the year."

"But I can ride about any horse here without any trouble!" exclaimed Tristan.

"That may be true, but this is the way I want it!" I was quite firm.

We got the ride out and I forgot all about the incident. I had other work to do.

The ride returned and Tristan looked somewhat ragged and a little dirtier than when he had left. I never did find out the full details of what happened, but what I pieced together was that Tristan had fallen off his horse because the horse had spooked at something. He had to almost bulldog the horse to keep him from coming home alone.

When I finally got Tristan alone, I asked him, "What happened?"

He didn't want to talk about it much and I didn't press him. But I did take the opportunity to impress upon him the fact that we were trying to keep the rides safe for everyone, guides included.

I did think it sorta funny that on the very ride that he objected to me sending out extra guides on, he fell off his horse!

I did, quite often, take the opportunity to tease Tristan when he rode that horse, by asking him, "Do you think we ought to send an extra guide along? You never know what's gonna happen!"

Of course Tristan didn't like that and I didn't know why. Was it because he might have to split a tip? Or was it because he didn't like my teasing him about falling off his horse on a ride that he thought he could handle himself?

I'm thinking it was because he might have to split a tip. After all, he was majoring in finance in college!

Instructions Ain't All that was Twisted

I generally give fairly complete instructions to all our new help when they show up. We go through the training sessions pretty regularly, so there's no reason why the new hired help shouldn't get it right.

I pay particular attention to the proper way to get on a horse. Most folks don't do it right, having done it wrong all their lives or watching the television cowboy stars get on wrong. I also show the hands how to cheek a horse.

To cheek a horse, a feller simply takes a hold of the cheek piece on the bridle with his left hand, pulls the horse's head into his side, puts his foot in the stirrup and gets on. A feller does have to be careful! If the horse does get his head down and starts to buck, he could pull the rider right under his front feet. The idea in cheeking a horse is to keep his head up so he can't buck and the rider can get on as safe as possible.

I show this to all the hands because even the old dude horses can be difficult to get on when the rider has gotten off to get something a rider has dropped. The horses don't like to be left behind! The proper way to get on a horse, when not cheeking him, is to stand by the horse's left shoulder, facing his rump, hold the reins in the left hand, take a mane hold with the left hand, turn the stirrup clockwise, put the left foot in the stirrup, take a hold of the horn with the right hand and swing on up. I'm real careful to show this to everyone and have everyone on the crew do it. They generally don't continue to do it during the summer, reverting back to their more familiar ways after the training session. But, they have been shown, and if anything happens it won't be because they didn't know.

It is kinda fun to watch them try the proper way after doing it wrong for so many years or perhaps never having gotten on a horse. A lot of people don't have any swing in them at all.

One particular individual had a particularly tough time mastering the method. I watched him get on one day to take out a two-hour ride and I noticed he turned the stirrup counter-clockwise rather than clockwise. I was about to tell him, but was called away. By the time I got back, the ride had left.

I didn't think any more of it until the ride returned. I was out by the corrals ready to help the tourists off when our hand that twisted the stirrup wrong came riding up.

"I didn't think getting on this horse your way was going to be painful for two hours!" he said to me.

"What seems to be the problem?" I already knew. I could see the stirrup still twisted wrong.

"I've had a terrible pain in my leg ever since we left. I must have pulled a muscle or something."

"That ain't your problem," I said. "Your problem is that you twisted the stirrup the wrong way and it's been rubbing you for the last two hours! Most people would have corrected the situation when they first noticed something was wrong."

"I didn't know," came the meek reply. "It sure was uncomfortable!"

"I'll bet," I said, as I turned to leave and have a good laugh. "You had it twisted backward!"

Gathering Horses?

Our rental horse outfit in Grand Lake, Colorado, had rented a ranch where we could pasture our horses that needed a rest or had become lame. It was pretty handy, only about three or four miles from the stable.

The outfit had a Continental Divide ride that came over the top of Rocky Mountain National Park from Estes Park to Grand Lake in August. The ride would take ten or twelve hours, depending on how well the riders kept their horses up and how long they would take for a noon meal. When they arrived in Grand Lake, where I was the stable manager, we would unsaddle the horses and I would trailer them to the ranch we had rented and turn them loose.

It was a fairly rough ride from the Estes Park side to Grand Lake and turning the horses loose would give them a chance to rest up some and get ready for the hunting season a month or so later. The ride was rough enough that they required the participants to have some riding experience behind them and kids under twelve were not allowed to go. Watching some of the riders get off their horses when they arrived in Grand Lake made me question just how much prior riding experience these people actually did have.

But the ride had been completed and I really didn't have any need to question the riders about their prior experience. Besides, now they had plenty more experience than they did when they started.

I always watched the horses when I turned them loose in the pasture. I didn't know any of the horses, as they had been at another stable all summer, and I thought it might be a good idea to know how many horses and what kind we had when it came time to gather the pasture. Some of the horses would run off as fast as they could when they were turned loose, others would walk off a couple of yards and just start eating.

I always thought that the horses would prefer the fresh grass to the baled hay, and even though it was becoming late in the summer, the grass was still fresh and good. I figured those horses that ran off just didn't want to work anymore.

When it came time to gather the horses and haul them to Craig, Colorado, for the hunting season, I took two other hands and we set out to gather the horse pasture. I left the office in capable hands with enough guides to handle what little business I was expecting. I didn't think it would be a tough job and as it turned out, it wasn't. There was a good corral at the south end of the pasture and we'd get the horses in it, and then trail them up the highway to the stables in Grand Lake.

"We'll put the horses in this corral, then trail them to the stables. I'll take the big circle and probably come up the bottom through the willows. You guys start to the sides and if you bring what horses you find to the corral, then wait in the gate so they don't escape, we should get all of them. Make sure you move out of the gate if you see any horses coming out of the willows. Those willows are so thick, I won't be able to see how many horses I have or what direction they're goin'. You might be able to see me from the side hills, so holler if you see any horses get behind me."

Instructions given, we started out. I didn't really like the idea of riding through the willows. The ground was boggy, swampy, and wet. There were some places where a horse would put his foot down and a feller could watch the ground ripple out in front of him. It was one of those areas where a guy might wish he was riding an eight hundred pound horse that wore a number three shoe. I took this route myself because I only wanted to gather this pasture once.

The gather went well, and occasionally I could see the rears of the horses in front of me. The willows were mighty thick and it was only rarely I could see any part of a horse. I never heard the other hands holler at me, so I assumed the horses were headed in the right direction.

I did see a dark gray leg through the willows, but I couldn't remember a horse that particular color. I didn't pay much attention to it, as it had been close to dark when I'd unloaded a lot of the horses.

I was trying to make sure the horses were ahead of me, while watching the ground ripple out in front of me. The footing was getting a little more solid and the willows beginning to thin out. I knew we were getting close to the corral. I was fairly wet from my horse splashing water up on me. It would be good to be on solid ground.

We broke out in the open and I was surprised. The gray leg I had been following turned out to be a big bull moose! And he was just following the horses that were about twenty yards ahead of him.

"Get out of the gate," I hollered. "We'll put the moose in there with the horses!"

My helpers were in the gate. They didn't move until I hollered. They were busy watching the moose.

The moose turned off, snorted and went back in the willows. The horses were corralled and the gate closed.

One of the hands asked, "Why didn't you try to head that moose off?"

"Well," I said. "I was thinking seriously of doin' just that, but when I hollered, he'd already made up his mind. If you'd have got out of the gate, he'd have just followed the horses in. I about had him trail broke!"

We counted our horses, and they were all there.

I gave instructions again. "I'll lead the horses home. You come with me an' peel off at the highway an' turn 'em up the highway. After they've all turned, come back, get the truck an' trailer an' follow 'em home. Use your blinkers on the highway to slow down traffic behind us.

"You," I said to the other hand, "follow along an' bring up the stragglers. We'll go at a trot, but don't run 'em over me. We got plenty of time. We're already ahead of schedule."

We took the horses back to the stable with out any problems. Our horse gather was a success, but I really would have liked to have brought in that bull moose with them!

Improper Procedure

Our new cook wanted to get horseback a little more often than he had. He'd been told that he could guide some of our rides in his spare time and he'd been here about two weeks and hadn't got on a horse. He was getting a little upset and kept asking me when he could go. He assured me he'd done a lot of riding.

The wranglers and I were trying out some new horses just to see what we had. They were already fitted to a saddle. Some of the horses had acted like they had a little bronc in them and we certainly wanted to know what they were like before we started renting them out at our rental horse stable. We had plenty of horses to try, so when the cook came down and wanted to help, I thought it would be a good time to get him on a horse.

These horses had been bought during the previous winter and they'd been rode, but we didn't know how they would act.

"You can ride that gray horse if you want," I said to the cook. "I don't know what he's like, that's what we're findin' out. He's been fitted to a bridle, its hangin' on the horn."

I gave him a mare to ride and purposely called her a him. The cook didn't notice.

I watched the cook as he untied the bridle from the saddle horn. I wasn't too impressed with the way he straightened the bridle out, but he did it.

I had some customers to take care of, so I had to leave for a little while. I told everyone to ride the horses they had in the big pen.

When I returned, the cook was riding the gray horse in the big pen, but the horse was fighting her head some. It looked like the horse was goin' where the horse wanted to go, rather than where the cook wanted her to go.

Too tight a rein, I thought, as I glanced at them. Then I corrected myself. *There's something else wrong!*

I called the cook over. "How's this horse?" I could see what was wrong as the cook got closer. And I didn't like it.

"He'll be all right," replied the cook. "He's a good horse."

"She seems to be fightin' her head," I said.

"Is this a mare?" The cook seemed a little surprised.

"Yes, she is." I said. "You might want to get off an' put that bridle on right."

"What's wrong with it?"

"Well," I said as the cook got off the horse, "you've got the curb strap in the horse's mouth! That ain't the proper way to bridle a horse!"

I was gettin' a little peeved at this guy, but couldn't get too mad—good cooks are hard to come by. And this cook did a good job.

"I'm sure you've made a mistake before in your life! I've bridled hundreds of horses before!" he said.

The cook was starting to get a little peeved also. I guess the tone of voice I used when I told him what was wrong wasn't very complementary. But I was also still upset.

"Yes," I replied, "I have made mistakes, but I haven't done anything that stupid since I was a kid!"

The cook bridled the horse and got back on. The horse acted about half decent, but still tossed her head some.

"Ride her with a looser rein an' she'll probably walk right out," I said.

Our somewhat heated exchange over the bridling earlier in the day brought an apology from the cook later on, over the noon meal. It also brought an exceptional meal from the cook!

Days Off

For some reason or another, I always try to give one hundred percent in everything I try to do. I wish we could hire help that tried to do the same.

In giving one hundred percent, I have come to take a great deal of interest in whatever business I am involved in. At the Moraine Park Stables in Rocky Mountain National Park, shortly after my arrival some years ago, I was made barn boss, and because of my position, I suppose, I took a greater interest in the business. Actually, I was somewhat reluctant to accept the position; I had sorta looked forward to a summer of simply guiding rides and not really becoming involved in management.

I had been involved in management of a horse rental stable for many years at my own stables and prior to that in Grand Lake, Colorado. I've come to the conclusion that the real job of a boss is simply to do all the things the hired help doesn't want to do. Consequently, the boss actually does more than the hired help and doesn't get credit for it. Most of the hired help thinks it's easy to be the boss as "he don't do nothin'."

For the last number of years I have gone to work on my day off to help saddle the sixty or seventy head of horses we planned on using that day. After these horses were saddled, the hay was put out and the first ride would leave, then it was time to start my "free" time. Generally it would be between nine and ten o'clock before I could get away.

Dave, my boss, had told me I should show up on my days off. He needed the help, and in his words, "We need to set the example for these youngsters!"

I set the example for a number of years and only once did an employee, Tristan, show up voluntarily on his day off to help saddle. He only did it once; he never again came in on his day off unless he was told to.

On one occasion on my day off, I heard a resounding crack in the corral. I knew what had happened; a horse had gotten kicked and got her leg broken. I got Dave, as he had already gone to the house, and informed him of what had happened.

Dave got some Bute, a tranquilizer, gave the mare a shot, and we started coaxing her toward the horse trailer. This happened toward the end of the summer and we were starting to haul horses out for hunting camp, so we got some other horses loaded into the trailer, coaxed the crippled mare into the trailer, and sent them to the farm.

Even though it was my day off, the stable had to operate, and I was the only one to run it. Pat, one of the employees, came up to me and said, "It's your day off, why don't you leave?"

"I can't," I answered. "Who's goin' to answer the phone, sign up rides, take reservations, assign horses an' send rides out? The job still has to be done."

Dave got back around noon. "You can start your day off now," he said.

Dave would generally assign days off in accordance with the anticipated needs of the company. Tuesday, Wednesday, and Thursday tended to be the busiest days of the week, with Saturday and Sunday most commonly the slowest. Monday was generally my day off, and this was good because a feller can't get a lot of business done on the weekends because everything's closed.

Before leaving on my day off, I would always tell Dave something to the effect, "Have a good day!" or "At least make my wages today!"

Regardless of Dave's planning, he always seemed to have a good day on my day off. When I would return for supper, I would ask him, "How did your day go?"

For a while, his answer was, "Very good!" Sometimes, "Excellent!" We tended to measure our days in terms of dollars.

I was getting somewhat concerned with the company making so much money, doing so well on my day off that I had to come up with some explanations, mostly for myself. When Dave's reply to my question at supper, "How'd your day go?" became "You know," I knew I had to do something.

One day, when his answer to my question was, "Exceptional!" followed by a number, which I knew referred to thousands rather than hundreds of dollars made, I volunteered, "I could take tomorrow off for the good of the company!"

"Hah!" Dave's reply was quite short and adamant.

I never did tell Dave that a lot of the business he did on my day off was due to the reservations I had taken during the previous week. His business acumen was such that he should have already been aware of that. We had already discussed the matter of days off and the effects upon the day's business and concluded it was a guessing game.

On another occasion when the company had done exceptionally well on my day off, I told Dave, "You know, I'm responsible for that!"

"How's that?" Dave was curious.

"You know I'm tellin' people to show up on my day off so I don't have to work so hard!"

"Hah!" Dave's reply was a curious mixture of humor and disbelief.

On another occasion, when Dave had an exceptional day on my day off, we equaled the amount of money made on the next day.

"That's a really good day," said Dave.

"Yes," I said. "We could have done more than what you did on my day off, but I didn't want to hurt your feelings!"

We discussed the days-off situation frequently and always came to the same conclusion, it was a guessing game.

One day, while discussing the situation about days off, I remarked, "It certainly is interesting how we banter back an' forth about how much we make on my day off, isn't it? I've had a lot of fun with it. It is all in good fun, isn't it?"

Dave didn't reply and I still don't know!

Bob

When new help shows up, my first question to them is, "How much horse experience do you have?"

I don't do the hiring, that's all done in March or April from the main office. Occasionally, I'll hire someone after the season has started, but the main part of the hiring is done before I even show up for the season. Consequently, I don't know what to expect of the hired help.

Most of the time the folks are fairly honest in assessing their horsemanship skills, although it seems most folks tend to overestimate their abilities. Such was the case with Bob. I haven't changed the names to protect the guilty.

When he showed up and I asked him the question, his reply was, "Quite a bit, but I haven't done it for four or five years."

When I hear "I haven't done it for so many years," I don't really hear that. I've been through this so many times in the past and when I hear that, a warning goes off in my mind that says what he's really saying is, "Actually, I don't have much experience, but I'm making my excuses now for all the mistakes I'm goin' to make in the future!"

This proved to be true with Bob. The next morning I was watching the crew halter horses in preparation for saddling, and watching Bob in particular. The boss, Dave, was watching with me.

"What' he doing?" Dave asked.

Bob had a horse caught, but was having a hard time figuring out how the halter worked. I don't think he knew what opening the horse's nose went into. It was a simple web halter.

"I think he's haltering that horse," I replied to Dave's question. "But I think the halter's winnin'!"

"He's been at it ten or fifteen minutes," Dave said.

"I could go help him," I said, "but I'm kinda enjoyin' watchin' the show."

"You better go help him. At the rate he's going, by the time we get the horses saddled, it'll be time to unsaddle. Looks like today will be a good day for training. You can't do too much training!"

I started into the corral to halter the horse, but someone else beat me to it. *Training,* I thought. *Can't do too much training an' it looks like I'll have to do a lot! Not only today, but in the days to come.*

It took Bob a good fifteen minutes or longer to figure out how a simple web halter works, and even longer to figure out how a rope halter works.

Bob wasn't much help in the saddling room either. He was pretty slow to start with and he didn't know how to tie the knot used in fastening the latigo to the "D" rings on the saddle. I ended up telling him, "If you get in my way, I'm goin' to run you over!"

When we got done saddling, we went right into training; from catching and haltering a horse to saddling and helping people get on. We were to repeat this many times during the beginning of the summer. In our training sessions, everyone that wasn't out on a ride participated. The more we trained, the better everyone got, although Bob was not picking up on things as fast as I thought he should, especially for someone who had done this "quite a bit."

Dave had to take the truck to a shop in Estes Park for servicing and he asked me who I could send to bring him back. We'd finished our training, so I suggested that Bob follow him in the town car.

Bob brought Dave back and we started another session of training. After a few hours, the shop called that the truck was ready.

"Who can you send to bring the car back when I pick up the truck?" Dave was pretty prompt about getting our equipment back.

I looked over the hands that were still at the stable.

"Take Bob," I said.

"NO! I've had enough of his bull!" Dave was quite adamant about it. "He never did shut up!"

I sent someone else. I never told Dave, but that was the reason I sent Bob in the first place; I had got tired of his bull and it was only his first full day!

After a few days, Dave asked me, "What kind of rider is he?"

"Well," I said, "I guess he can ride. I sent him an' Ben out to clear some trail an' he come back at a full trot carryin' a shovel on that new horse."

Dave frowned. Moving a horse out of a walk was frowned upon, especially when headed home. That reinforces a horse's desire to come back to the corral faster than we might want him to, thereby creating the possibility of a runaway. Not a good thing with inexperienced riders.

"Make sure he walks that horse! He might create more problems than we want!" Dave was quite adamant about it.

We had to unsaddle some horses, but for some reason or other we couldn't run them through the saddling chute we normally

R Lovin
SCHMIDT "Bring the
Baldy"

used. Bob caught one of the horses, tied him to the corral (I had to show him the knot I'd showed everyone earlier in the day) and stepped back to survey the situation. I was watching from the other side of the corral.

Bob promptly approached the horse on the right side, the "off side," and went to pulling on the off billet. Immediately I went to Bob and stopped the procedure.

"Everything is done from the near side, that is, the horse's left side!" I continued, "You'll cause an awful lot of confusion for everyone else by doin' it wrong. And we don't have time to be correctin' your mistakes!" I was starting to become a little short tempered with Bob. For someone who had done this "quite a bit," he wasn't using any skills he should have acquired.

Bob didn't have any horse equipment of his own, but that's all right; we had plenty of saddles and other equipment. And we did give Bob a new saddle to use. He was honored, but he didn't know we gave it to him because we wanted him to break it in.

It wasn't too many days later when Bob came back from town with a new pair of chink chaps. I never asked him what he paid for them, but he was fairly proud of them. They certainly looked better than my old pair, which had been used fairly roughly on a regular basis.

A new hand showed up late in May and she turned out to be a pretty good hand. Bob had left his new chaps in the barn overnight and the new girl was admiring them.

"Whose chaps are these?" she asked.

"Their mine," replied Bob. Then he volunteered, "I wear them every day."

I heard this and almost fell over laughing. The new girl didn't know he'd bought them only three days ago! I wondered just how much longer he would try to pull the wool over everyone's eyes. The more he tried to impress, the more he showed his own inexperience!

Even though I showed everyone how to get on a horse properly, Bob still struggled. I found it particularly humorous just watching him. While he did try to incorporate some of what I had showed him in this procedure, it didn't always work right. After he'd made plenty of mistakes, sometimes sliding back to the ground, he'd look over at me to see if I'd seen him. I had, but I never really said anything for fear of further embarrassing him. He'd embarrassed himself enough.

We continued training and the other hands seemed to be progressing, but Bob still struggled. He really wasn't mentally incompetent, but I think he did get instructions mixed up, or simply didn't pay attention.

Part of our job is to help the dudes—guests that is—get mounted. This can be quite a chore, especially if there's fifteen or sixteen people going on the ride. Bob was a good talker—he did that better than anything else! All too often he'd help somebody on a horse, then stand there gossiping with them. I caught parts of some of these conversations and from what I could tell, it didn't amount to anything except bull! There was plenty of that!

More than once I had to holler over to him, "That gal is all right! Go get someone else on!"

One of our cardinal rules is that a guide never put someone on a horse with the horse still tied to the rail. The first time Bob did this, I quietly slipped up to him, untied the horse and told him, "We don't do that."

I'd covered the topic quite extensively more than once during our training sessions.

"I'm sorry," said Bob.

The second time he did it, I lost it. I told Bob exactly what I thought of him, his experience, his parents, and his line of bull. It's a shame I can't repeat it here, it was quite colorful!

That's really not a good thing to do in front of the tourists going on a ride. It doesn't help build confidence in the tourist to let them know just how incompetent their guide really is. It certainly doesn't add to an enjoyable ride for the guest.

Bob again said, "I'm sorry."

And I let everybody know just how sorry he was! I got on him so bad that I didn't dare send him on that ride, so I sent someone else.

Even with the apparent embarrassment, the lesson didn't sink in. Bob's next episode with someone getting on a horse while still tied to the rail occurred a week later as he was getting ready to take a ride out.

I watched as he prepared to get on his horse. He knew I was watching and I suppose he tried to do it right. He didn't get it exactly right, but he was successful! He got on his horse!

However, he made one mistake. He forgot to untie his own horse from the rail! There he was sitting on his horse, but his horse wasn't going where he wanted him to. After a while surveying the situation, he figured out what was wrong.

I guess he knew how hard it was for him to get into the saddle, so he tried to right the situation without getting down. He stayed in the saddle and tried to reach the halter rope by standing up in the stirrups and reaching down.

He made quite a sight, his butt sticking up in the air, his head down by the horse's shoulder and his hands reaching for the lead rope. He finally gave up and got off and untied his horse, wiping sweat from his forehead.

I know the horse Bob was riding and I also know that he wouldn't put up with that maneuver if I tried it. The horse did have a reputation for bucking people off in his younger days and he was certainly still capable of it. I suppose somebody really is looking out for fools or whatever.

Bob did have a wreck. I wasn't on the ride so I can't say for sure what happened. But I was told that the horse Bob was riding, a big gray gelding, spooked and started to run off. Bob

R. LOREN
SCHMIDT.

dropped his reins and grabbed the saddle horn with both hands. Of course he didn't have any control over the horse and no way of even slowing him down. Apparently the horse ran next to or under a tree and Bob was brushed off. When he hit the ground, he broke a couple of ribs and punctured a lung. We had to have the Park Service extradite him to the hospital.

Bob was gone a surprisingly short period of time. He returned to work a couple of weeks later claiming he was ready to go back to work. But he wasn't. He had never been real fast to start a chore, but after his wreck he was even slower.

For some reason or other, Bob had to leave early, before the season was over, to take care of some family matters. I was somewhat relieved. To my way of thinking, when Bob was on a ride, it was just another person the guides had to look after. I never did ask the other help what they thought, but we did all have some good laughs over some of his antics.

I was telling Dave how relieved I was that Bob had left and made the comment, "I think the rest of the help is a little more at ease now that he's gone. They're certainly payin' more attention to the dudes out on the trail. I guess a serious wreck is what it takes."

"It's unfortunate that he had that wreck," replied Dave, "but if that's what it takes, then he was good for something!"

Sometime later, when Dave had returned from taking some horses out, he was sorting out halters that had just been tossed in the back of the truck.

"You look like Bob sortin' them halters," I said, as I came up to give him a hand.

"Good thing for you I don't have my gun handy," Dave replied.

The next time I caught Dave sorting halters, I cautiously asked, "Is your gun handy?"

We both laughed because we both knew what I was referring to. I suppose Bob was good for something else—we could both grin over some of Bob's antics although it may not have been so funny at the time.

Don't Lose Your Horse

A cowboy afoot is a pretty sad sight. Cowboys belong on their horses unless they're doing some sort of ground work like branding, ear marking, castrating, or some kind of doctoring. Fixing fence is a different matter, depending on the outfit a feller is working for.

On some outfits, particularly out in Nevada, where a feller is hired as a buckaroo, he's not expected to get off his horse other than for the ear marking, castrating, or doctoring. If he's out fixing fence, all he does is knock the staples in on the top wire and if the fence is down, he rides back to camp or the ranch and tells the cow boss, who in turn tells the farm manager and the farm manager sends out a fencing crew to fix the fence right. On other outfits, a cowboy is expected to do it all, from fixing fence to fixing the truck or whatever else needs fixing. I never did like hiring on to those outfits where a feller did his riding in the morning, and then somebody put a shovel in his hand or told him to go change the water.

Regardless of where I was working, whenever I got off my horse, the first thing I did was hobble my horse so I didn't have to walk home or back to camp. I learned this lesson the hard way, having to walk back to camp because I thought my horse would ground tie. It only took one long walk back to camp to learn the lesson, but I learned it well.

I learned it so well that one time when I had to work the gate while we were sorting cows and calves in a corral that I got off my horse, hobbled him, then to make sure he wouldn't leave, I loosely wrapped the reins around the top pole of the corral. Later, something spooked him and he pulled back. He didn't go anywhere as he was hobbled, but he did bust the fancy chain I had from the bit to the rein. Another lesson learned, but at some expense.

I had just bought an expensive half breed bit with the chain attached to the rein and was using it that day. It didn't look so fancy with some baling twine swinging where the chain should have been on that fancy bit. I was kinda embarrassed and fixed it as soon as I got back to the ranch, even before I had supper.

These days, there's too many distractions to a horse to just leave him ground tied and expect him to be there when a feller is done with his work. The same is especially true in the rental horse business.

The dude horses know the trail and they know when they get back they're generally done for a while or for the rest of the day. Unfortunately, in the dude business, a wrangler has to get off his horse quite often to check cinches, adjust stirrups, pick up a camera or a hat or other items, or occasionally, a dude.

Learning how to do this stuff and holding onto a horse can be difficult, particularly if a feller is new. Most folks just turn the horse loose, expecting him to stay close to the other horses, or thinking, "The horse likes me and he won't go anywhere." Most of the time they do stay close, but quite often, especially if they're close to home, they'll go home.

Dave, our boss at Moraine Park Stables in Rocky Mountain National Park, is quite adamant about holding onto your horse out on the trail. One time, apparently, a guide's horse got loose and started for home and ran right through a ride that was headed out. About ten or twelve riders—dudes—lost their horses when the riderless horse passed them and the dude horses wheeled around and followed him to the barn. The incident was not lost on Dave, and every year at some point during the orientation speech, he would mention it and generally add, "Such a happening is grounds for immediate dismissal!" Dave was serious, and most of the help took him serious.

However, some of the help never did get the hang of hanging onto their horses, feeling like they needed two hands to do whatever they were doing. Over the years, I've seen guides turn their horses loose numerous times.

When I've seen this, I've told the guide, "Better hold onto your horse! He'll go home without you!"

"Oh, he'll be all right." Their answer would generally be matched with a loving glance at the horse peacefully grazing along the trail. Sometimes they would add, "He wouldn't leave me!"

Quite often I would slip up and catch the horse and hold it for the guide until they completed whatever it was they were doing. And, quite often, I would detect a triumphant look in the guide's eyes as they mounted, as if to say, "See, I told you so!"

However, one incident didn't turn out so well. It was on the very first ride I went on at Moraine Park Stables. I went on this ride just to learn the trail, as I had never been on it before. If I remember right, there were nine or ten guests on the ride. Arturo was the lead guide and I was just along to learn the trail and to be of assistance if necessary.

Arturo was having some problems with a woman toward the front of the ride. She kept dropping items and complaining about her stirrups. Arturo had to get off his horse five or six times to retrieve items she had dropped, and vainly tried to adjust her stirrups to her comfort. I don't think the woman ever got comfortable. I knew Arturo got quite upset at this woman and all that he had to do for her. At one point, when he picked up her camera for the seemingly umpteenth time, he told the woman, "I'll just hang this on my saddle horn so you don't lose it again!"

He didn't give the woman a chance to object—he just hung the camera on his saddle, mounted, and started to lead the ride on.

Arturo had to get off again to adjust the woman's stirrups, and just turned his horse loose. The horse, knowing we were headed home and knowing we were close, just started walking down the trail, leaving Arturo afoot.

I had been riding up along side the ride to see if I could give Arturo a hand, and I saw Arturo's horse leave for home. I hurried to see if I could head the horse off, and as I passed Arturo, I heard him complaining about losing his job because his horse had left him. He was complaining loud enough that the woman who gave him such a hard time could hear him.

Later, I thought it might have been just a ploy to try to get a bigger tip out of the woman. He wasn't the least bit bashful about voicing his displeasure and how hard he had to work on the ride.

I did catch his horse down the trail a couple of hundred yards. As I approached Arturo leading his horse, I could still hear him complaining. I gave him his horse, and he actually seemed more upset that he had the horse. He was not having a good day!

He took the horse without as much as a thanks, got on and started to lead the ride home. I didn't even get a thanks for catching his horse *and* maybe even saving his job! Knowing what I know now, I should have caught the horse, led him back to the barn, and let Arturo walk back in. It's true he probably would have lost his job, but it would have alleviated a lot of problems later.

I had learned my lesson many years previously. Arturo didn't seem to learn his lesson, as he kept turning his horse loose when he had to get off and help someone.

The Players

We meet a lot of people in the rental horse business, some of them are pretty regular people and some of them are a little strange, both as customers and as hired help.

One year we had two girls named Paige working for us, so we had to differentiate the girls by naming them Paige One and Paige Two.

Paige One had some previous stable experience, having worked at one of our stables in Arizona. I had depended on her quite a bit in the beginning, but as the summer wore on, she seemed to lose a lot of her interest in the job and I didn't think her as capable as I did originally. She ended up leaving before her contract was up and forfeited her end of season bonus. I kinda hated to see her go as she had been pretty fair help, and losing her bonus meant a fairly sizeable monetary loss for her.

Paige Two was a different story. When I asked her how much horse experience she'd had, she simply shrugged her shoulders and extended her hands out with her palms up. I took this to mean none, and I was right.

But Paige Two turned out to be the most improved wrangler of the summer. I guess when you start at the bottom the only way to go is up. As it turned out, she became a pretty good rider, but certainly not a bronc rider. She paid close attention to the tourists and their needs and didn't create extra problems.

She did have a problem with her boots. One night she couldn't get one of her boots off. I lent her my bootjack but that didn't work. She told me that she'd work on it and I went to bed thinking she'd get them off eventually.

I found out the next day that she hadn't gotten the boot off. She'd showered in it, slept in it, worked and rode in it all day. It had to be mighty uncomfortable.

That night, she asked me for some help in getting the boot off. The bootjack didn't work again and with some misgivings, I told her I could cut the boot off. She went for that idea and I got out my pocketknife.

Actually I had to borrow a sharper knife. I'd cut too many strings with my knife and it wasn't sharp enough to cut Paige Two's boot tops.

Very carefully I cut the boot top along the side of Paige Two's leg. I had to be careful; I didn't want to cut her! I finally got the boot cut from the top enough so Paige could get her foot out. What had happened was that the inside lining of the boot had come lose and when Paige Two tried to get her foot out, the lining balled up against her heel and she couldn't get herself freed.

Paige Two was quite relieved to have her foot free and wasn't too bashful about thanking me. I was careful to tell her, "Now don't you go thinkin' you're a bronc rider 'cause you have your boot cut."

"What do you mean?" She looked perplexed.

"Well," I said, "them bronc riders in the rodeos, the professionals, they cut their boot tops like I did yours. That way, if they get bucked off an' hung up in a stirrup, they can get loose before they get dragged."

"Oh! I don't think you'll have to worry about me becoming a bronc rider, even if I have some of the equipment," she said.

Paige Two made it through the rest of the summer with one boot split without having to get on any broncs.

Kylee was a pretty good-looking wrangler from Texas. She'd had quite a bit of riding experience previously, and I came to count upon her quite a bit. She did get bucked off during the summer, but she was tough and kept right on working. I never could figure out Kylee's laugh; I couldn't determine if she was choking or if we had a mule braying. But she did sit a horse well.

Jake was a wrangler I couldn't quite figure out. I guess he'd had some riding experience in the past, but I'd have liked to have seen more experience. He didn't seem to show any fear around the horses and I don't know if he was fearless or just didn't know anything. I'm inclined to believe the latter. I know he was pretty rough on our horses, so Dave generally had him riding the knotheads.

Jake also seemed to be in a constant state of wonder. Almost everything he saw was new to him and he almost seemed to be studying it all. More than one comment was made about him "being out there."

I don't know how it came about, but at supper one night, Jake was marveling about how far we had come in the last fifty years or so. Quite a realization considering he was only about twenty-one or -two.

"We've come a long way," Jake said. "We've got intercontinental ballistic missiles; we can put a man on the moon, that's really something! In my lifetime we might even be living on the moon!" Jake was getting a little excited.

"Just think," he continued, "We might be living on the moon and become space cowboys! What do you think of that, Dave?"

Dave wasn't near as excited as Jake. "You already are," he answered.

Dave and I immediately broke into a hearty laugh. I almost choked on the food in my mouth. The comment went right over Jake's head.

One thing all the help had in common was forgetfulness. Dave kept his horses in a separate pen and when their water got low, we'd have to run a hose from the water tap to his water trough to fill up the trough. I kept a pretty close eye on the level of water in the trough and even though it only needed to be filled about every three days, I checked it every day.

I would send someone out to clean Dave's pen every day and remind them to check the water. Invariably the water would be neglected, and I would have to have someone fill the trough during the day even when the corral had been cleaned earlier in the morning. It became a necessity that I check the water every day.

I always told the help to hook up the automatic water valve back to the tap when they were done filling Dave's tank. They would hook up the automatic water valve back to the tap, but for some reason or another, they wouldn't turn the water back on. A few hours later, I would notice a few horses putting their heads pretty deep into their water trough and I would have to go turn the water back on.

It finally occurred to me that I hadn't told them to turn the water back on after they had filled Dave's water trough and hooked up the automatic water valve! Maybe I'm a little forgetful also!

There were some other people that worked for us the summer of 2011, but unless they did something really outstanding or really stupid, I tend to forget them.

Duder

When I owned my own horse rental stable, I was always on the lookout for good horses. And I wanted to buy them cheap. I was willing to give a fair price, but the horses couldn't cost me much money. There were two very good reasons for this. First, the cheaper I could buy the horses, the larger my profit margin would be and second, I didn't have much money!

I was more interested in disposition and conformation than color or breed, although colorful horses are always more popular at rental horse stables. But I've heard some people tell their horses that they were beautiful even though I personally thought the horses were downright ugly.

I heard about a woman who had a horse for sale and she wasn't asking much money for the horse. I got the information and made arrangements to meet the gal and look at the horse. I put my saddle in the truck and went out to look at the horse. I also brought my checkbook along. It doesn't do any good to try and buy something without any money!

I had some misgivings about the mare, as I really wanted geldings. And when I finally saw the horse I was kinda surprised. The horse's feet needed trimming and shoeing real bad, but otherwise the horse was well cared for. Too well cared for! The horse was fat, too fat to go right to work. I figured I could only use her an hour or two a day until she lost some weight. To use her more than that might endanger her health, she was that fat.

I also had the thought that I could buy her at the price the gal was asking, take her to the sale and double my money by selling her to the killer buyers. This was before horse slaughter was outlawed. A lot of horses were killed for meat purposes and their carcasses shipped overseas and used for human consumption in countries like Japan, Belgium, and France.

While the thought had crossed my mind, I didn't really want to send the horse to the killers. She was a nice little mare with a good disposition and a nice conformation, if she lost some weight. If she was an easy keeper, as I suspected she was, I could see a fairly moderate feed bill for her during the winter.

We had to discuss the sale terms.

"What do you want for the horse?"

I knew her asking price, but wanted to make sure we were on the same page.

"I want four hundred dollars for the horse."

We talked about the horse for a while and I picked up all four feet. She seemed gentle as a kitten.

"What are her bad habits?"

"She doesn't have any," she replied. "She's a real sweetheart!"

I asked her, "Why are you selling her?"

There's a reason why every horse is sold and sometimes it's not a very good reason.

"I need the money," was the reply. "And I'm so busy, I don't have the time to ride her and enjoy her."

"Do you know you could probably take her to the sale and get considerably more than that for her? The killer buyers would probably give you double what you want for her, as fat as she is. And the killer market is what sets the base price for everything."

I was being real honest with the gal. I didn't know if she knew what her options were. And while I wanted to buy the horse, I didn't want to steal it.

"I don't want to have the horse killed," she answered. "What will you do with the horse if I sell her to you?"

"As fat as that horse is, I could only use her for about an hour a day until she lost some weight and got into better shape. I'll give you the four hundred for her but you have to furnish a brand inspection on her. I'll give you a check for the four hundred now an' you call me when you have the brand inspection an' I'll bring the horse trailer an' pick her up, if that's all right with you."

"I guess I could go for that," she said.

I wrote out a check for four hundred dollars and gave her the phone number of the brand inspector and my phone number. We shook hands and I figured I had bought another horse for our dude string. And, I was so favorably impressed with the horse and the gal that I bought the horse without riding it!

I left and while driving back to the stables, I felt pretty proud of myself. I had bought another horse, the price was reasonable, and I felt the mare would work into our operation nicely. I felt I had dealt with the woman professionally and fairly, and I felt good about that because I wanted to bring some creditability into the horse-rental business in the county.

I felt really good about the deal, until the next morning. We were just getting ready to send out our first ride of the day when the gal burst into my office, waving my check over her head and yelling something about me being a two-faced horse trader and some other things I won't repeat here. She ripped up my check and threw it on the counter, then turned around and stomped out of my office.

My customers were shocked and I was totally taken back. I told my customers I was trying to buy a horse from her and apparently she had changed her mind. But changing her mind certainly didn't require a demonstration like she had just put on.

I sent the ride out and tried to figure out why the horse deal had gone sour. The only reason I could come up with was that she couldn't get a legal brand inspection. I let the matter settle, as there wasn't anything I could do and didn't give it much thought afterward.

A few weeks later my good friend, Steve Mantle, showed up to shoe some horses for me. I was discussing old times with Steve while he was shoeing and I mentioned the incident with the woman and the horse I thought I had bought but didn't.

"I haven't figured out why that gal was so upset. I gave her the asking price and only wanted a brand inspection to make the deal legal," I said.

"Well," said Steve as he straightened up and stretched, "that's really pretty simple."

"It's a mystery to me," I said.

"No, it's simple," stated Steve. "She doesn't know you, right?"

"Right."

"She doesn't know what you do, right?"

"That's right," I replied.

"It's that simple."

"I don't see it," I said.

"It's simple. She found out you're a duder! Stu, you know some folks think a stable horse has a tough life being saddled and tied up all the time and being ridden by amateurs. She was mad that you didn't tell her that you're a duder!

Mixing Up the Sexes

Sometimes in today's world what we see isn't always what we get. For example, a twelve-ounce steak in some restaurants looks more like a six-ounce steak in other restaurants to me. Or a "clearance sale" where the prices are actually jacked up a few dollars; that's not what I expected.

The same is true in the dude business. The guy that walks up to our stable dressed in three hundred dollar boots, two hundred dollar spurs, new pants, and an expensive shirt topped off with a straw hat that looks like it's been through a hay baler, which he actually bought that way, is probably trying to impress everyone with his horse expertise. If the truth were known, he probably doesn't have any horse experience, probably more money than sense.

It seems like to me in this business that the more a person tries to tell how much he knows about horses, the more I find out how little he really knows. I've been around horses most all my life and there's hardly a day goes by that I don't learn something new.

One of these fancy-dressed persons was sitting by our corral one day as I walked by, and he asked, "When is that gelding going to have her colt?"

I was taken back by the question for a number of reasons. Number one, geldings can't have colts; they're males that have been castrated. Number two, I wasn't aware that any of the mares were pregnant, and number three, I was surprised by the stupidity of the question.

So I asked the man, "Which one do you mean?"

"That one, over there," he said, pointing out in the corral.

"You mean the sorrel?" I had stopped, more curious than anything.

"The one that looks like she's red in color," he said.

I looked out in the corral. The only horse that was red was Moses. Moses was a mustang that was a real easy keeper. He stayed pretty fat without much feed. But he sure wasn't fat enough to be pregnant.

"Well," I said, "that's Moses. He's a sorrel. I guess he'll foal in a couple of days."

My answer went right over the guy's head. He completely missed my reference to Moses as being a "he."

"Don't you think you ought to separate him from the others?"

The dude was now referring to Moses as a "he," but seemed to be unable to accept the fact that "he" wasn't going to give birth.

"He should be all right," I said, stressing the "he." "I think he's done it before."

I was thinking I'd like to have a little fun. The feller seemed to be oblivious to everything except that Moses was kinda fat. Unfortunately, I couldn't continue the fun; I had to get a ride out.

But the dudes aren't the only ones that get the sexes mixed up. I've done it myself and more than once. I've done it more with people than horses, but it's happened both ways.

I remember one family, a couple of kids and Mom and Dad. I took them to the rail to assign horses. I gave the dad his horse and one of the hired hands started to get him on his horse. I did

R. LOREN
SCHMIDT.
"MONTANA Cowboy"

the same with one of the kids and someone else helped him on. All I had left was the mom and the last kid.

"Now, young lady, you'll ride this horse we call Sarge." I started to tell the youngster that Sarge was my granddaughter's favorite horse, when the youngster interrupted me.

"I'M A BOY!" The youngster was quite adamant about it.

I didn't know what to say, and without thinking, I said, "Well, get a haircut! You're almost as cute as my granddaughter!"

Now, we're not in this business to insult our customers, no matter what their age is. Insulting customers is a cardinal sin and I thought I had just committed it.

But I was vindicated when Mom instantly hollered, "Yes!" She was in agreement with me!   ❖